Tacca · Se

Michela C. Tacca

Seeing Objects

The Structure of Visual Representation

27|Ⅷ|2013

*Ad Alberto
con affetto,
M.*

mentis
PADERBORN

Gedruckt mit Unterstützung des Förderungs- und Beihilfefonds Wissenschaft der VG Wort.

Einbandabbildung: © juanjo tugores – Fotolia.com

Bibliografische Information der Deutschen Nationalbibliothek

Die Deutsche Nationalbibliothek verzeichnet diese Publikation
in der Deutschen Nationalbibliografie; detaillierte
bibliografische Daten sind im Internet über
http://dnb.d-nb.de abrufbar.

Gedruckt auf umweltfreundlichem, chlorfrei gebleichtem
und alterungsbeständigem Papier ⊚ ISO 9706

© 2010 mentis Verlag GmbH
Schulze-Delitzsch-Straße 19, D-33100 Paderborn
www.mentis.de

Printed in Germany
Einbandgestaltung: Anne Nitsche, Dülmen (www.junit-netzwerk.de)
Satz: Rhema – Tim Doherty, Münster [ChH] (www.rhema-verlag.de)
Druck: AZ Druck und Datentechnik GmbH, Kempten
ISBN 978-3-89785-709-4

Table of Contents

Acknowledgements

The idea behind this book manifested when I was a doctoral student at the University of Siena. This book is the revised version of the dissertation that resulted from the development of that basic idea, and I am very grateful to those who supported me during this project. Sandro Nannini introduced me to the importance of philosophical analysis in cognitive science, and, at the same time, to how much philosophy can benefit from other disciplines. Andreas K. Engel, Alexander Maye, and Till Schneider had the patience to teach me how scientists work, and to involve me in very interesting experiments, when I was a visiting student at the University of Hamburg.

This work could not have been the same without the numerous comments received during its gestating and developmental periods. I particularly thank Brian P. McLaughlin for his invaluable comments on the first draft of the book-to-be, while I was a visiting student at the Department of Philosophy and Center for Cognitive Science at Rutgers University. I also would like to thank Tobias H. Donner and Thomas Papathomas for reading and commenting part of this work. They saved me from the common philosophical error to describe the visual system in a way that fits better one's own ideas. It turned out to be a hard task that I deeply enjoyed.

Helpful discussions on the topic of the book are still going on with Gerhard Schurz and Markus Werning at the Heinrich-Heine-University of Dusseldorf.

Excerpts of this work were presented at meetings at the University of Siena, the University of Dusseldorf, the CUNY Graduate Center, the ESSP conference, and VAF IV conference. I am grateful to the participants of those meetings for their helpful comments.

Finally, I am particularly grateful to my husband, Tobias, who supported me at each stage of this long process.

Research for this work was supported by a studentship of the Volkswagen Foundation (AZ II/80 609), and a post-doctoral stipend by the DFG (FOR 600).

Al mattino presto in queste pianure la luce è tutta assorbita dai colori del suolo. C'è un vapore azzurrino che fa svanire le distanze, e oltre un certo raggio si capisce soltanto che le cose sono là, disperse nello spazio. È col sole alto e la luce netta che cominciano a vedersi grandi separazioni.

(Gianni Celati, *Verso la foce*)

Introduction

Natural visual scenes typically confront us with a variety of distinct objects (Marr, 1982), each of which is defined by the combination of several elementary features such as color, motion, and shape. Furthermore, the various objects in a scene are arranged according to lawful spatial relations (Palmer, 1977; Kanizsa, 1979; Edelman, 2002), the representation of which we exploit for recognizing objects, understanding scenes, and planning actions. We know that the visual system represents object features in separate areas, such that every object is decomposed into primitive features (i.e., color, motion, orientation, size, spatial frequency) that are recombined only at later stages of visual processing. For example, a scene with a bucket full of apples is decomposed into, as a simple approximation, brown, red, round, vertical, and so on. These features, then, have to be recombined so that the red apples and the bucket are correctly represented. Given the segregated nature of the visual system and the absence of association areas in it, the explanation of how percepts become unified assumes the dimension of a problem. This problem is known in vision science as the *binding problem* (Hardcastle, 1994; Treisman, 1996). The binding problem in vision refers to how the visual system binds primitive features to coherently represent objects.

The problem of how our mind ties together the varieties of information coming from the senses has been studied in philosophy since at least the seventeenth century. For example, Locke (1690) argued that perceptions, as 'complex ideas', must be created by compounding 'simple ideas' of sense both within and across modalities. It is in part because we can experience the simple ideas of RED[1] and SMOOTH that we can perceive, for example, the apple as being both red and smooth. Kant (1787; Kitcher, 1990) stated that the synthesis of perception (i.e., the unification of sensory experience) is achieved only through the active role of the mind in integrating the ongoing flow of sensory information. In other words, perceptual synthesis occurs at a late conceptual, not an early sensory level.

The notion of the synthesis of visual experience as a conceptual process, gathering information from sensory processes, is also endorsed in works of philosophy of mind (Evans, 1982; Peacocke, 1992a). Following Frege (1879, 1918), these works maintain that the conceptual level is *essentially* structured (Evans 1982, pp. 100–105). Thoughts seem to be related according to their similarity of contents: The ability to entertain the thought *aRb* is related to the ability to entertain the thought *bRa*. In fact, those thoughts involve the same conceptual abilities:

---

[1] I follow the common practice in philosophy of capitalizing terms that refer to mental representations.

The abilities to think about $\underline{a}$, $\underline{b}$, and the relation $\underline{R}$ (McLaughlin, 2009). The structure of thought is sometimes coupled with the Language of Thought Theory (LOT; Fodor, 1975). According to LOT, the constituents of the thought 'John loves Mary' – 'John', 'Loves', and 'Mary' – are bound according to the syntactic rule ⟨subject-verb-object⟩, so that 'John' and 'Mary' play different causal roles in this thought. This particular language-like structure allows for recombining constituents into different configurations, and avoids the binding problem that derives from simultaneously activating primitive constituents of a complex configuration (Fodor and McLaughlin, 1990). A pervasive property of such a process is its systematicity (Fodor and Pylyshyn, 1988); that is, the ability to entertain structurally related thoughts: An individual that can think aRb can also think bRa. Moreover, systematicity involves compositionality. According to the principle of compositionality, the content of a complex thought, such as aRb, is determined by the content of its constituents and the way they combine. Specifically, thoughts are compositional because the constituents contribute with the same content in every systematic recombination (Fodor, 1998a). Hence, if a system has a compositional structure of constituents, then it is also systematic.

Compositionality and systematicity are pervasive features of higher-level cognitive processes, such as thought processes, but do not apply to sensory processes, such as visual processes. According to the Generality Constraint (Evans, 1982, pp. 100–105), a thought is systematic only if the subject that entertains that thought is able to entertain structurally related thoughts. The requirements of the Generality Constraint are met only if a subject possesses the concepts involved in the thought. According to this view, object identification cannot be possible without a basic kind of conceptual knowledge. In addition to that, according to LOT, a systematic and compositional structure of constituents results from language-like processes on conceptual representations. Thus, architectures that implement cognitive processes according to different rules, such as artificial and natural neural networks, fail to have a systematic and compositional structure of constituents (Fodor and McLaughlin, 1990; McLaughlin, 1993a, 1993b; Fodor, 1996). Because visual sensory processes are parallel and distributed processes on non-conceptual representations, the processes underlying object representation and recognition are not systematically structured (Fodor, 2007).

Both the arguments for the conceptual nature of visual conscious experience and vision to be an unstructured system can be challenged. On the one hand, recent philosophical studies provide reasons for the non-conceptual nature of visual conscious experience by analyzing the differences between vision and thought: *(i)* Vision and thought have different structures (Heck, 2007); *(ii)* the content of visual representations is more fine-grained than the content of thought representations (Evans, 1982; Peacocke, 1998; Kelly, 2001; Tye, 2006); *(iii)* visual experience cannot sometimes be influenced by our beliefs (Jackson, 1977; Crane, 1992a).

On the other hand, results from perceptual psychology and neuroscience suggest that the synthesis of our visual perception is achieved *within* the visual system; that is, at the sensory level (Roskies, 1999). The majority of these studies have focused on how elementary features are bound into objects; that is to say, they have focused on visual feature binding. Studies of visual feature binding provide evidence for the structured nature of vision. The visual system consists of several dozen distinct cortical areas (Felleman and Van Essen, 1991). Early and intermediate level areas contain topographic maps of the visual field (Wandell *et al.*, 2007); each of these maps seems to be specialized for a specific feature (Zeki, 1978; Treisman, 1993). A specialized area that completely recombines all these distributed representations of features does not seem to exist. Nevertheless, features are properly combined in our perception. Thus, an active and flexible binding mechanism is required. An influential model postulates that visual attention accomplishes this binding by selecting the features occupying the same location throughout all feature maps (Treisman and Gelade, 1980; Reynolds and Desimone, 1999; Robertson, 2003). This selection might be mediated by the synchronization of neuronal activity (Crick and Koch, 1990; Fries *et al.*, 2001; Siegel *et al.*, 2008). The process of visual feature binding is, thus, a combination of primitive visual constituents (i.e., features) with non-conceptual content.

The active role of attention in binding primitive visual features and, thus, securing the representation of objects was already pointed out by Condillac (1980). He suggested that, without actively attending to the objects in a visual scene, information contained in that scene could not be properly bound. To imagine how the loss of binding can occur, Condillac proposed the following thought experiment (as we would call it today): A group of people arrives to a castle on top of a mountain at night, thus, missing the chance to see the beautiful panorama from the castle's windows. At sunrise, the windows are open only for an instant, and the visitors can experience part of the panorama. Condillac suggested that, because of the brevity of the experience, the visitors cannot attend to things in the panorama (houses, fields, trees, and so on), and, thus, they can only experience simple features at distinct locations, rather than coherent objects. Therefore, the visitors cannot recognize the objects in the panorama without actively attending to it. Condillac's thought experiment transposed into contemporary research describes the role of attention in binding features occurring at the same location.

Given that compositionality and systematicity are central topics in the study of cognition, it appears reasonable to consider whether the structure of visual feature binding, as described by psychophysical and neurophysiological findings, is compositional and systematic. There are some characteristics that neuronal mechanisms that implements a compositional and systematic structure of constituents have to possess in order to bypass the difficulties raised by classical cognitive models (Bienenstock and Geman, 1995):

(1) Dynamical binding (*first-order binding*): The sensory representation of composite entities has to include the representation of patterns of neural activity that correspond to the constituents of those entities. The ability to dynamically recombine the same primitive constituents in order to allow structurally related representations avoids a *superposition catastrophe* (von der Malsburg, 1987) that derives from the inability of neural networks to distinguish between structurally related representations. The implementation of dynamical binding processes results in the implementation of a compositional and systematic structure of constituents.

(2) Relational binding (*second-order binding*): The ability to bind constituents according to their causal role in the representational process. Relational binding is qualified in terms of collections of domain-specific relations among constituents. For example, the representation of 'John loves Mary' has to specify that 'John' and 'Mary' are predicates of the two-place relation 'Loves', and that 'John' plays the subject-role and 'Mary' the object-role.

(3) Hierarchical computation: Compositional cognitive representations are hierarchically organized. Hence, compositional sensory processes are expected to be hierarchically organized, too.

Some parallel distribute models implement (1)–(3) (e.g., Werning, 2003; Frank *et al.*, 2009). For what concerns perceptual representations, structural models of object recognition (Biederman, 1987; Hummel & Biederman, 1992; Hummel, 2000) describe object representations as deriving from the combination of primitive symbolic constituents processed in a parallel-distributed fashion. The result is that structural models display systematicity.

In this work we propose an alternative to the study of neural compositionality by considering the spatial structure underlying visual binding operations. This model, different from structural models of object recognition, does not require a classical symbolic architecture. My general neurophilosophical approach (Churchland P.S., 1986) will be to integrate insights into the neural basis of visual binding with philosophical theories of the properties of structured representations. Specifically, I will assess whether the visual representation system is, like conceptual representation systems, systematic and compositional, and so whether visual representations, like conceptual representations, have a structure of constituents that satisfies (1)–(3). Reasons why I decided to specifically focus on visual feature binding are given from the fact that vision is one of the most studied systems in psychology and neuroscience. Psychophysical and neurophysiological findings provide a wealth of knowledge, specifically about the processes underlying object representation and recognition. Moreover, the level at which feature binding occurs is 'non-cognitive', namely, it belongs to early sensory processes that are unlikely to be effected by higher-level cognitive processes. This last condition is important to rule out the influence of higher-level processes on binding operations, and, thus, to attribute to higher cognition any of the properties of object representation. Rather, those properties are intrinsic properties of the binding processes occurring within the visual system.

The plan of this work is as follows:

Chapter one is about the non-conceptual nature of visual experience. First, I describe how the word 'looks' can be interpreted and argue that the phenomenal use of 'looks', as described by Jackson (1977), contains a rudimentary notion of the non-conceptual nature of visual experience. I, then, consider the arguments for the existence of non-conceptual representations at both the sensory and conscious levels.

Chapter two is about the compositionality, systematicity, and productivity of cognitive systems. I, specifically, focus on Fodor's Language of Thought theory, and start to build up a theory of compositionality (syntactic compositionality) that will turn to be necessary to explain the compositionality of visual binding operations. I also describe the requirements that a system has to meet to be a systematic system, and how systematicity relates to the binding problem.

Chapter three presents the binding problem in vision from psychophysical and neurophysiological perspectives. I describe the different types of binding – the binding across feature dimensions and the binding of elementary features across space – by considering the possible mechanisms that underlie them. Among those mechanisms, I argue that the hypothesis of binding by attention has the better chances to explain how the binding problem is solved.

Chapter four is about the systematicity of vision. In order to evaluate whether binding operations are systematic, it is necessary to determine whether structurally related visual scenes involve recombinations of the same primitive visual constituents. I take into consideration three different kinds of binding: *(i)* binding across feature dimensions; *(ii)* binding of elementary features across space (i.e., perceptual grouping); and *(iii)* binding of objects according to their spatial relations. *(i)* and *(ii)* fall within the category of, the so-called, *first-order binding*, whereas *(iii)* is defined as *second-order binding*. I argue that the representation of objects' locations plays a fundamental role in the explanation of how objects' features are combined within vision, and that the process of feature binding is systematic.

Chapter five is about the compositional structure of vision. I consider the requirements vision has to meet to be a compositional system. It turns out that the compositionality of the binding processes underlying visual object representation is better explained in terms of syntactic compositionality. This directly follows from the characterization of visual object representation as depending on the binding of non-conceptual representations.

Chapter six considers a general outcome of my analysis of vision as a systematic and compositional system. Against Evans' justification of the Generality Constraint within the *fundamental* level of thought, I propose that the systematic structure of (at least) perceptual thoughts mirrors the systematic structure of the sensory processes that underlie object representations.

I conclude that vision, as a parallel distributed and hierarchical system, has a systematic and compositional structure of constituents. I, thus, provide an explanation of 'neural compositionality' that satisfies (1)–(3). Hence, against a common tradition in philosophy of mind, I argue that systematicity and compositionality are not only pervasive features of higher-cognitive systems but also pervasive features of sensory processes operating on non-conceptual representations. I am also convinced that, more generally, my work provides the initial instruments to trace the relations between the study of vision and the study of thinking.

1
The Non-Conceptual Content of Visual Experience

I am looking outside the kitchen window: There is the usual traffic jam in the Brooklyn-Queens Expressway; people are playing basketball down in the playground; and the Empire State Building is turning red at sunset. One might think that it is quite a boring scenario and I might even agree with that. However, it seems that even if there is nothing special in the scene itself, there is something special in my experiencing it. Particularly, it seems that I cannot be able to capture all the details in the scene that I am experiencing just by describing it: The Empire State Building is turning red but I do not exactly know how to describe that particular shade of red. I could say that it is a mix of orange and pink but I would not thereby express the completely determinate shade of color that I am experiencing. I can perceive the actual determinate color of the Empire State Building without having a concept of it. Sensory experiences (in this case visual experiences) can have a finer content than the subject of the experience can describe. Thus, visual experiences (and sense experiences in other modalities as well) represent the world in ways that do not require the bearer of the representations to possess the concepts required to specify their content. To take a further example, something can look red and right angled to someone who lacks the concept of red and the concept of something's being right angled, for example, a very young child. Visual experiences are for this reason claimed to have non-conceptual representational contents. A mental state has a non-conceptual content if and only if the subject of the state needs not to possess the concepts that would be required to specify the content of the mental state. Whether any mental states in fact have non-conceptual content is a controversial issue. Before considering further the arguments that support the thesis that visual (and other sense) experiences have non-conceptual content, I will first describe three senses of the word 'looks' and highlight which of these senses seems to characterize a visual experience by its non-conceptual content.

1.1 Three Senses of the Word 'Looks'

Roderick Chisholm (1957, ch. 4) and later Frank Jackson (1977, ch. 2) distinguished three ways the word 'looks' (and 'appears') is used to talk about visual experience: *(i)* The epistemic use – 'It looks as if p' –; *(ii)* the comparative use – 'It looks like an F' –; and *(iii)* the phenomenal use – 'Something looks F to S' –.[1]

Roughly, if we consider the three uses of 'looks' in terms of conceptual and non-conceptual contents, then it turns out that, on the one hand, the epistemic locution presupposes the possession of conceptual representations in order to experience something as if P; on the other hand, the phenomenal locution attributes states with non-conceptual content to a subject's experience. Instead, the comparative use of the world 'looks' cannot be sharply defined by following the distinction between conceptual and non-conceptual contents of the visual experience.

The epistemic use of 'looks' has the following form: 'It looks as if p', where p is a proposition. It seems that something cannot look as if p unless a subject has the concept P. Consider, for example, the sentence 'It looks as if we are the last ones to leave the restaurant', where the statement following *as if* expresses the proposition p. This sentence expresses facts about the situation appearing in a certain way: If we are in the restaurant, and it turns to be empty after some time, then our visual experience supports the statement 'It looks as if we are the last ones leaving the restaurant'. However, there are cases in which it can look to me as if p, and yet p be false. Suppose that the waiter comes to our table and tells us that in that particular restaurant they have two dinner-shifts: The first one is already over, and the waiters are cleaning the room before the second shift starts. In this case, 'It looks as if we are the last ones to leave the restaurant' turns to be false. Particularly, the proposition p, supported by our visual experience, is now disconfirmed by other sources of evidence (i. e., the words of the waiter). Hence, epistemic locutions can be evaluated according to their semantic value.

However, the fact that epistemic locutions can be evaluated according to their semantic value is not sufficient to claim that the epistemic use of 'looks' involves concept possession. In fact, some authors argue that also non-conceptual mental states can be true or false (see, for example, Crane, 1992a). Rather, in order to evaluate whether the epistemic use involves concept possession, we need to focus on the fact that an epistemic locution describes a visual experience as a *representation as*. For something to look as if it is p, it is necessary that the object of the experience falls under the appropriate concept P. Let us consider a simpler

---

[1] The variables p and F have different values in the three uses of 'looks'. In the epistemic use, p expresses a proposition; in the comparative use, F expresses indefinite singular terms; and in the phenomenal use, F expresses a sensory property (Tye, 2000, ch. 3).

example than the restaurant one, namely, a visual scene with a red apple:[2] For something to look *as* if there is a red apple, we need to possess the concepts RED and APPLE. The possession of those concepts is necessary to represent the object in the scene as that specific object. In contrast, to have a visual experience of an apple does not seem to involve concept possession: One can see an apple without the need to possess the concept APPLE. Of course, one needs to possess the proper concept, in order to say that there is an apple but this is not the issue here. Here, I am only considering whether a subject needs to posses a concept in order to epistemically, comparatively, and phenomenally experience the world. So far, it seems that the epistemic use of 'looks' involves concept possession. This is because the epistemic sense entails the *representation* of visual states of affairs *as* those particular states of affairs.

Notice that the epistemic use of 'looks' – It looks as if p – does not entail to believe that p. There can be cases in which something looks as if p to a subject without the subject believing that is p. For example, it can look to a subject as if the Sun is revolving around the Earth without her actually believing it. Thus, in the epistemic case, it can look to one as if p, and yet one not believe that p.

As opposed to the epistemic use of 'looks', the phenomenal sense – 'It looks F to me', in which the value of F explicitly expresses terms for colors[3], distances and shapes – seems to involve the description of visual experiences with non-conceptual representational contents. One can infer the argument for the non-conceptual nature of visual experience, as described by the phenomenal locutions, by considering Jackson's defense against the reduction of the phenomenal locutions to epistemic (Pitcher, 1971) and comparative senses (Chisholm, 1957). The phenomenal expressions, "'It looks *blue* to me', 'It looks *triangular*', 'The tree looks *closer than* the house', 'The top line looks *longer than* the bottom line', 'There looks to be a *red square* in the middle of the white wall', and so on (Jackson, 1977, p. 33)," cannot be arguably reduced to, and explained in terms of, comparative and epistemic expressions.

In order to distinguish between the phenomenal and the comparative use, let us compare the phenomenal sentence 'It looks red to me' with the comparative sentence 'It looks like a red thing usually looks to me in normal conditions'. Jackson argues that *(i)* 'It looks red to me' can be true when 'X looks like a red

---

[2] The difference between the two examples is as follows: In the restaurant example, the statement 'it looks as if p' is satisfied in an indirect way, namely, its satisfaction depends on the evaluation of the perceptual evidence that, for example, there are no people in the restaurant, the waiters are cleaning, and so on. Instead, in the apple example, the statement 'it looks as if p' is satisfied in a direct way, namely, the experience of p, as the apple, depends on the direct experience of the apple.

[3] There are cases in which the uses of 'It looks F to me' are not phenomenal. These are the cases in which F does not express a sensory property, such as, for example, 'It looks edible to me', 'It looks impossible to me', and so on.

thing usually looks to me in normal conditions' is false; and *(ii)* 'It looks red to me' can be false when 'It looks like a red thing usually looks to me in normal conditions' is true. Based on this distinction, he claims that the phenomenal use cannot be reduced to the comparative one. In order to clarify matters, let us consider a few examples of these uses of 'looks'. First, consider the case where 'It looks red to me' is true and 'It looks like a red thing usually looks to me in normal conditions' is false. This is the case in which "there might be a shade of red which objects look to have at sunset but which no object actually has (Jackson, 1977, p. 37)." In this situation a subject may perceive something to look red to her, but it would not be true that she perceives something that looks like a red thing to her in normal condition, since there is no such a color under normal conditions. Now, consider, instead, the case where 'It looks red to me' is false and 'It looks as a red thing usually looks to me in normal conditions' is true. Jackson's example is of a color-blind person who can only perceive the world through different shades of gray. Each of those shades corresponds to a color in the normal colors' spectrum, although the color-blind person cannot perceive the normal spectrum of colors. In this situation, this person is able to express 'It looks as a red thing usually looks to me in normal conditions' because red corresponds to a particular shade of gray in her color spectrum. On the contrary, the sentence 'It looks red to me' is false because she can perceive only shades of gray. Instead, to express a true statement about her phenomenal experience, she would have to say: 'X looks like a particular shade of gray to me'.

The phenomenal use of 'looks' does not seem to be reducible to epistemic terms such as, for example, belief terms (Jackson, 1977, pp. 37–48). The main argument to support the distinction between the phenomenal use and the epistemic one is that there are cases in which believing does not entail looking, and, conversely, cases in which looking does not entail believing.

The first argument – believing does not entail perceiving – can be spelled out as follows:[4]

> I can believe (or retain the belief, or acquire the belief, or causally-receive the belief) that there is, say, something red in front of me without anything looking red to me or it is looking to me that there is something red before me. (Jackson, 1977, p. 42).

This condition describes, for example, a situation in which a person believes that there is a red object right in front of her, although she cannot see it. She can entertain this belief for many different reasons: Because she knows which objects are in that particular room, and she is able to locate them, although she does not see them; because someone else told her about that red object in the room; or

---

[4] Jackson's argument is mainly aimed to criticize theories that describe perception through beliefs (like, for example, Pitcher, 1971). According to these theories, beliefs involve perception: If a person believes something, then something looks that way to her.

because she has a map of the room that describes that particular red object at that particular position.

The second argument – perceiving does not entail believing – is a counterexample to the case in which to experience something as being true involves that the related belief is true. Consider, for example, the Mueller-Lyer illusion (i.e., the perception of two doubled-head arrows, depicted one on top of the other, as being of different lengths): A subject that is unaware of facing an illusion can believe that what she perceives is true, namely, that the two arrows are of the same length. This subject is not going to believe anymore that the arrows have the same length, once she knows that the arrows are actually of the same length:[5] She will still experience the illusion (i.e., the arrows as having different sizes) but her previous belief about the arrows having different lengths turns now to be false. This example supports the claim that the truth of 'It looks p to me' does not entail that 'I believe that p' is true.[6] That is to say, something can look F to one, even if one does not believe that it is F.

A major problem that Jackson's account faces is related to the link between the phenomenal sense of 'looks' and the idea that whenever we experience something being F, the object of our experience is a sense-datum. A sense-datum is: *(i)* The immediate object of perception; *(ii)* a 'patch' that represents color, distance, and shape; and *(iii)* the bearer of the apparent properties. Thus, whenever a subject perceives, for example, something to look red to her, a red sense-datum occurs. This sense-datum is the immediate object of one's perception, and its properties coincide with the properties of the object in the world, but, at the same time, a sense-datum is a mental object. That is to say, sense-data are the ending product of a long chain of inferences that starts with raw information about objects and ends with the representation of object properties by means of a sense-datum. Evidence for the existence of sense-data, as mental objects, are given by considering hallucinations:

> It is sometimes urged that it is part of the meaning of the world 'hallucination' that then someone is under an hallucination he is not seeing anything at all, and so that is simply a matter of definition that visual hallucinations are not physical things. [...] As far as the definition is concerned, there may be pink rat-like (mental) shapes which are seen by drunkards, and there may have been a mental image seen by Macbeth which he mistakenly took to be a dagger (Jackson, 1977, p. 51).

---

[5] In principle, a subject could come to believe again that the two arrows have the same length. This could happen only if the subject forgets about the illusion, namely, when she does not know anymore that the arrows are drawn in such a way to look of different sizes.

[6] As already noted, the epistemic use of 'looks' does not always involve 'believing that p': Something can look to a subject as if p, without her believing that p. I think that the same applies to the comparative use as well.

Sense-data theories have been criticized on the basis of different arguments, like, for example, that sense data do not fit into a physicalist account of mental states, and that sense-data theories lead to skeptical arguments about the existence of physical objects. Nevertheless, despite the reference to sense-data, Jackson's account posits the basis for recent works on the non-conceptual nature of visual experience.

For what presented so far, it emerges that the phenomenal use of 'looks' is distinct from the epistemic and comparative uses. Particularly, as opposed to the epistemic sense, 'It looks F to me' does not seem to involve the possession of the concept F. In fact, it seems that, whilst we cannot experience something *as if p* unless we have the concept P, we can experience something to look F without possessing the related concept. Moreover, the phenomenal use is arguably belief-independent: The visual experience of something looking F does not necessarily involve that the related belief is true. Belief-independency is considered to be one of the fundamental properties of non-conceptual representational content (Evans, 1982). Before considering the arguments for the non-conceptual nature of visual experience, let me open a parenthesis and, briefly, motivate why I think that the comparative sense of the word 'looks' cannot be sharply defined in terms of conceptual and non-conceptual contents.

The comparative use of 'looks' includes expressions of the form 'It looks like an F', where F expresses indefinite singular terms. These expressions, 'It looks like a cow', 'It looks like a bent thing', 'It looks like an apple', are all included in the comparative use. The way things look to a subject in the comparative use also depends on the nature of the circumstances under which the subject perceives them. Hence, a proper definition of the comparative use is: 'It looks like an F does in certain circumstances to a subject', where subject refers to the subject of experience, and circumstances refer either to normal circumstances or to the circumstances obtained at the time of the sense experience. For example, the expression 'It looks like a bent thing does in daylight to me' refers to myself experiencing something in a specific circumstance.

It seems clear that if we consider a subject's thinking or uttering 'It looks like a bent thing does in daylight' the subject has to possess the required concepts in order to think or utter this sentence. However, what is interesting is to evaluate whether the visual experience described by the comparative use necessitates concept possession. Chisholm (1957) points out that any comparative sentence can be translated into sentences that describe properties of physical things. For example, the expression 'It looks like bent in daylight' can be translated into 'It looks the way a subject would expect a bent things to look in daylight'. In this sense, the subject cannot experience something like being bent without having expectations on how a bent thing looks during the day. But, the translation of comparative locutions in terms of subject's expectations requires concepts possession. On the contrary, one might argue that for something to look like a bent thing to a subject does not seem to involve concepts possession. A subject can experience a specific object in daylight without needing the related concept. The question, now, is: Can something to look like a bent thing does in daylight without the subject possessing the concepts of BENT and THINGS? The answer is yes, if we consider, as opposed to Jackson, 'It looks like a bent thing' to be equivalent to 'It looks bent to me'. In this case, it seems possible that for something to look like bent for someone it is not necessary to have the relevant concept. Given the possible use of the comparative sense to indicate either conceptual or non-conceptual visual experiences, it is not possible to sharply define the comparative use in terms of a specific representational content.

I can, now, close the parenthesis and sum up what presented so far. Even if Jackson does not explicitly refer to the non-conceptual content of visual experience in his work, I argue that the phenomenal use of the world 'looks', as opposed to the epistemic use and, perhaps, the comparative use, implicitly refers to a description of the visual experience as having non-conceptual representational content. The first author who has explicitly introduced non-conceptual content in this way is Evans (1982).

1.2 Why There is a Non-Conceptual Content

In *The Varieties of Reference* (1982), Evans defines perception as a part of an informational system that gathers, stores (through memory) and transmits (through communication) information about the world. Informational states are closely connected to thought: They provide the content on which thoughts are based. Specifically, the content of information-based thoughts (i. e., perceptual thoughts) includes information about objects acquired through perception. A paradigmatic example of perceptual thought is when one can identify an object by demonstrative referring to it. Perceptual demonstratives like, for example, 'This is an apple', 'That is a tree', 'This is a man', and so on, refer to and identify objects due to the information provided by the sensory systems. For example, in a pure case of a visual demonstrative (i. e., a demonstrative thought that solely depends on visual perception), the content of a thought depends on the information about the object gathered through vision: One can refer to the unknown man that is walking the dog, as 'That man', due to her visual experience of the man.

However, the information-link between the visual sensory system and demonstrative thoughts is not sufficient to secure an objective experience of an object, though it is necessary (Evans, 1982, ch. 6). According to a 'Kantian' definition of visual experience, object identification is possible only if a subject possesses basic conceptual abilities. Thus, visual sensory processes carry information that is necessary to distinguish objects in the world but not sufficient to objectively identify those objects. Consider, for example, a person that sees a man and recognize him as being Martin. Her thought about Martin includes both the information she gathers from actually seeing Martin, and her beliefs acquired during past encounters: Whenever this person sees Martin, she also has access to the fact that Martin lives in Berlin, is a doctor, and so on. The thought about Martin is information-based because it is caused by the perceived object, but it is not a pure case of information-based thought, since there is more in it than just the information obtained through the current perception. Specifically, in order to be able to entertain a 'non-pure' perceptual thought, a subject needs to be able to retain information about the perceived object even when the object is not available. From the fact, that a person is able to think about the identified object, it follows that this person can also entertain related thoughts that involve the same perceived object. In the example above, the person that identifies the man as Martin is also able to think that Martin is a doctor and lives in Berlin. The ability to entertain related thoughts about the same object is a major requirement for achieving proper identification. This ability is a fundamental property of thought, as described by the Generality Constraint (Evans, 1982, pp. 100–105).

The Generality Constraint requires that structurally related thoughts, such as *aRb* and *bRa*, involve the same abilities, namely, the abilities to think that *a* and *b*. The ability to entertain structured related thoughts involves concept possession: It is not possible to entertain indefinite thoughts about *a*, without possessing the concept a. The Generality Constraint, thus, differentiates the realm of sensory informational processes, which involves non-conceptual representations, from the realm of thought processes, which involves conceptual representations.

The idea that visual experience has non-conceptual representational content is based on the following considerations: *(i)* Visual experience is sometimes independent of what a subject believes; *(ii)* it seems to be a common feature in animal and human cognitive lives; and *(iii)* its content is finer-grained than the content of thought. These considerations fall within the *state view* (Heck, 2000), according to which an experience has non-conceptual content if *(a)* it has correctness conditions, and *(b)* a subject needs not to possess the concepts related to the experience to specify its correctness conditions. Notice that, the state view does not discriminate between the kinds of representational content (i.e., conceptual content vs. non-conceptual content) a visual experience has, because it is a condition on the possession of concepts. The state view claims that a subject's visual experience is not totally described by the concepts she possesses. Therefore, the state view leaves open whether some aspects of visual experience have conceptual content.

As opposed to the state view, the *content view* posits a stronger condition (Heck, 2000, 2007): It is the view that visual representations and cognitive representations have different contents. An example of argument supporting the content view is: *(iv)* Because vision and cognition are representational systems with different combinatorial structures, and because structural properties relate to semantic properties (Fodor, 1975), then visual representations and cognitive representations have different contents. *(iv)* has the major relevance for our analysis of the combinatorial structure of the processes that underlie visual object representation, and it is developed throughout this work.

1.2.1 *The state view*

Some features of our visual experience cannot be explained by our conceptual abilities. According to the state view, those features have to be explained by reference to the non-conceptual nature of visual representational states. Belief-independency is one of the cases that support the state view. Evidence about belief-independency of sense experience comes from visual illusory experience (Jackson, 1977; Evans, 1982; Crane, 1992a). Whenever a subject is aware of experiencing an illusion (like, for example, the Mueller-Lyer illusion), she cannot influence her perception of it by, for example, believing that her experience is false: The illusory experience remains the same, notwithstanding that the subject believes her experience to be false. If sense experience is independent from belief, then one can argue that the kinds of representation processed in the formation of belief and in sense experience are different. Particularly, these representations have different contents: Informational processes are operations on non-conceptual representations, while thought processes involve operations on conceptual representations. As Evans puts it:

> The informational states which a subject acquires through perception are non-conceptual, or non-conceptualized. Judgements based upon such states necessarily involve conceptualization: in moving from a perceptual experience to a judgement about the world (usually expressible in some verbal form), one will be exercising basic conceptual skills. But this formulation (in terms of moving from an experience to a judgement) must not be allowed to obscure the picture. Although the subject's judgements are based upon his experience (i.e., upon the unconceptualized information available to him), his judgements are not about the informational state. The process of conceptualization or judgement takes the subject from his being in one kind of informational state (with a content of a certain kind, namely, non-conceptual content) to his being in another kind of cognitive state (with a content of a different kind, namely, conceptual content). (Evans, 1982, p. 227).

Another difference between visual experience and cognition is that visual representations sometimes allow for contradictory experiences (Crane, 1988). This is the case, for example, of the, so-called, Waterfall Illusion: If we look for a period of time at a waterfall (moving downward), and then look at the trees beside it, the trees will appear to drift upward. Although the trees appear to move, they do not appear to move relative to the background. That is, since the trees appear to move we would expect them to change their positions relative to the background. Instead, we perceive the trees occupying their original positions as if they are not moving. This violates a basic principle about the rationality of our judgments, namely, we cannot judge or believe at the same time 'that p and *not p*'. However, visual experience seems not to conform to this assumption. Particularly, the waterfall illusion shows that it is possible to experience at the same time 'that p and not p'. Because perception is not subject to the principle of non-contradiction, as opposed to cognition, it seems hard to provide an explanation of sense experience in terms of conceptual representations. In fact, contradictory experiences argue against the involvement of any conceptual source in sense experience.

Conceptual and non-conceptual contents, thus, occupy different levels in the cognitive hierarchy: Thoughts depend on higher-level cognitive processes, in which reasoning and judgments take place; instead, visual sensory processes and visual experience depends on more primitive processes. Sensory processes occur at an early stage in which higher cognitive influence is absent. Early informational stages are what adults, infants, and 'higher-animals' have in common. This claim is nowadays related to what is called 'the autonomy thesis' (Bermúdez, 1994; Peacocke, 1994, 2002), according to which it is possible for organisms to have states with non-conceptual content even if they might lack a conceptual system (animals) or do not possess the adequate concepts yet (infants). It seems plausible to think that infants can perceive things in the same way adults do, although they probably have rough conceptual abilities, or maybe even lack some of them. For example, small children can see a computer like adults see it but they do not *see* it *as* a computer. For seeing a computer, children and adults just need to open their eyes but, then, their conceptual representation of a computer as a computer is different: Infants do not represent the square object they perceive as a computer.

Whether a non-conceptual system can exist independently of a conceptual system is matter of debate. For example, Evans refutes the hypothesis that visual conscious experience is fully non-conceptual, namely, that it does not require the possession of basic conceptual abilities. It follows that animals have a primitive form of perceptual experience that is distinct from the conscious identification that humans experience. In fact, visual conscious experience is possible only with the possession of some basic concepts, such as the concepts of an objective space (Here), and of self (I) (see Evans, 1982,ch. 6).[7]

A main argument for visual experience as a non-conceptual mental state is that the content of conceptual representations is too coarse for capturing the details represented in our experience. To fully capture the content of our experience, representations with a finer-grain content are necessary. A way to distinguish between representations with a fine-grain content and representations with a coarse content is to consider which information is carried by those representations. One can distinguish between an analog way and a digital way of encoding information

---

[7] A similar argument was developed by Peacocke (1994). Subsequently, he modified his view to support the autonomy thesis (Peacocke, 2002).

(Dretske, 1981; Peacocke, 1986). The analog way is related to sensory systems, whereas the digital way of encoding is related to higher cognitive systems such as language, belief, and thought. The digital encoding of information is a discrete state, which encodes only the relevant informational states. An example of digital system is the on/off button on the radio. Instead, the analog encoding of information is a continuous state, which encodes all the information about a state independently of its relevance. A picture is an example of analog information.

To see the differences between the analog and digital ways of encoding information, consider, for example, how the representation of a white rose is converted into digital and analog formats. The sentence 'a white rose' describes that there is a white rose. It does not supply us with any other information, such as, for example, whether the rose has thorns, a long stem, etc. On the opposite, a picture of a white rose depicts a white rose by showing the thorns, the length of the stem, the different shades of the petals' color, etc. In this case, the signal carries more specific information than the one included in the sentence 'a white rose'. Of course, a more complete description of the picture's content can be given in a digital way, too, but this can be done only with some loss of information (Kitcher and Varzi, 2000). The description of the picture representing a white rose can be something like: '(Petal $(y_1, ..., y_{40})$ & White $(y_1, ..., y_{40}))$ & (Stalk(x) & Green (x)) & (Thorn $(k_1, ..., k_{10})$ & Hunter Green $(k_1, ..., k_{10}))$ & On top of $(y_1, ..., y_{40}; x)$' & etc. It seems obvious that this description (and many similar ones) is not sufficient to capture all the details of the picture. The incompleteness of the description has to be attributed to the limit of our conceptual representational system. Consider again the picture of the white rose: We can clearly perceive that one of the thorns is broken such that its shape does not look triangular anymore. Even if we can perceive the particular shape of the broken thorn, we lack the word to describe it: Its shape can maybe resemble a trapezium, and yet trapezium is not the exact description of it. Thus, the picture provides us with richer information about its content; a richness of content that cannot be fully captured by our conceptual abilities. Therefore, the content of our visual experience has to be represented by a kind of representation that does not acquire information from our conceptual repertoire. This kind of representation is more primitive, insofar as it involves non-conceptual content.

At this point, one has two different options for determining the content of sense experience: Either one postulates a conceptual apparatus that can satisfy the richness of perceptual information or one identifies a specific kind of content for sense experience that does not depend on our conceptual ability. Evans rejects the attempts to reduce perceptual content to conceptual representations and identifies it with non-conceptual content:

> Further, no account of what it is to be in a non-conceptual informational state can be given in terms of dispositions to exercise concepts unless those concepts are assumed to be endlessly fine-grained; and does this make sense? Do we really understand the

proposal that we have as many colour concepts as there are shades of colour that we can sensibly discriminate? (Evans, 1982, p. 229).

The fine-grained nature of perceptual content has been matter of debate (McDowell, 1994, 1998a/b; Peacocke, 1998; Kelly, 2001). On the one hand, McDowell suggests that demonstrative thoughts, such as, for example, 'That Shade', 'That Size', and so on, can capture the content of sense experience as sharply as the non-conceptual representations postulated by Evans. The main argument is that in order to conceptually capture the richness of our sense experience we do not need to have a complete set of general concepts. Rather, it is enough to express sentences like, for example, 'That Shade', in which the demonstrative refers to a particular sample of the experience. Consider again the example of the white rose: One can describe the particular shade of white where one petal superimposes on another using the concept SHADE, even if one lacks the general concept for that particular type of white. However, this is a conceptual capacity only if we can put some *distance* between the expression of the concept and the perception of the object identified by the concept (McDowell, 1994, p. 57). 'Distance' means that one has to be able to recognize the same object if one comes again to perceive this object within a short period of time. Consider the case when someone perceives a specific shade of white – pearl white – and describes it as 'That Shade'. According to McDowell, a subject possesses the general concept SHADE only if she can recognize the same sample of color after a short period of time as being of the same shade.[8] This recognitional capacity is conceptual since the concept of a shade is enough to capture the details of our color experience. On the other hand, Kelly (2001) points out that this recognitional ability is not a valid condition on demonstrative concept possession. Kelly's example is as follows: Suppose one presents the same sample of color to a subject ten different times. The subject does not know that the samples have the same color, namely, pearl-white. Nevertheless, if one asks the subject if the presented samples were all of the same colors, she might correctly answer that all of them were of the same color. That is to say, the subject is able to indicate the samples as corresponding to 'That shade' of color. Then, following McDowell, one might conclude that the subject is able to recognize the sample of color corresponding to pearl-white. However, suppose, now, that in another experiment one shows to the same subject two samples with different colors. Again, the subject does not know that the two samples respectively correspond to off-white and pearl-white but she turns to be as good as she was in the previous experiment to discriminate between the color samples. However, it happens now that if one asks the subject whether the actual sample of pearl-white is of the same color as the sample of pearl-white

---

[8] The length of the interval between the two events is arbitrary. The only constraint is that the interval of time has to be long enough to consider it as a break between the two presentations.

one showed her in the previous experiment, she answers that the two pearl-white samples have different colors. At this point, it is not anymore clear whether the subject has recognized the samples, namely, if she possesses the general concept SHADE. Moreover, Peacocke (2001) argues that demonstrative thoughts cannot explain 'non-conceptual phenomena' because they imply general knowledge that we do not need to possess in order to perceive the world. For example, in the demonstrative thought That Shade, SHADE individuates a general concept. But neither do we need to have this general concept for perceiving shades nor do we need it to perceive an object as having the same shade. From this point of view, concept possession is not necessary for perception. Therefore, the content of our experience differs from the conceptual one, insofar as it is non-conceptual.

1.2.2 *The content view*

The main idea of the content view is to find a way to show that the content of visual experience is actually different from the content of cognition. An argument that can be included in this view derives from considering how the visual system represents objects in a visual scene.

According to an influential theory in philosophy, the Language of Thought Theory (Fodor, 1975), thoughts have a combinatorial structure of constituents that is the basis of every possible recombination of thought. A complex thought, such as, for example, the thought that John loves Mary depends on the combination of primitive representations (e. g., 'John', 'Loves', and 'Mary') according to specific syntactic rules. These rules are as such that every representation that is part of a complex representation is a proper constituent of the complex representation. To be a proper constituent involves playing a fundamental role in determining the content of the whole (Fodor, 2007). In this sense, not every kind of composition is allowed: For example, 'John loves Mary' has as its proper constituents 'John', 'Mary', 'Loves', 'John Loves' but not 'John … Mary'. On top of that, the rules of combination of thoughts are formal rules used in predicate logic.

Vision seems to lack this kind of combinatorial structure (Fodor, 2007; Heck, 2007): *(i)* Vision does not combine primitive representations by implementing a structure based on a formal grammar; and *(ii)* the visual representation of objects depends on the spatial configuration of objects' constituents. *(ii)* is particularly important, since it seems that, because of the spatial nature of visual combinatorial processes, vision does not have a structure of proper constituents. That is to say, the decomposition of an object representation into its primitive constituents admits an unlimited number of possible constituents, since there are no formal and semantic rules that constrain the causal role of visual constituents. Given that syntax and semantics are tightly related to determine the content of a complex representation, from the fact that vision and thought have different syntactic and semantic structures, it follows that vision and thought have different representational contents. On the one hand, thoughts involve processes on conceptual representations. On the other hand, vision involves processes on non-conceptual representations.

I agree with this argument that vision and thought have different structures, and that structural differences might involve a difference in content. However, as I will extensively describe in this work, I disagree with the idea that from the fact that vision does not implement a constituent structure that depends on language-like processes it follows that vision lacks a structure of proper constituents.

1.3 The Content of Visual Representations

I have so far introduced several arguments to support the existence of visual representations with non-conceptual content. Now, it is necessary to define which is the information that such content represents and which are the conditions under which non-conceptual content is satisfied.

According to Evans, visual experience carries information both about object features and object location. The representation of an object location provides a subject with a description of the world surrounding her. This description is given in an egocentric reference frame: The position of an object is calculated on the basis of its relative distance and position from the subject's body. The way in which humans and animals acquire this specific kind of information depends on a complicated network made up of perceptions and actions. Perception is linked to behavior, such that behavior co-varies according to changes in stimulus: "We can say, then, that auditory input [i.e., sensory input] – or rather that complex property of auditory input which encodes the direction of sound – acquires a (non-conceptual) spatial *content* for an organism by being linked with behavioural output in, presumably, an advantageous way (Evans, 1982, p. 156, *italics GE*)."[9]

Thus, perception provides organisms with sufficient information for behaving in the world. But, is the link between perception and behavior enough for an organism to have conscious experience? In Evans' account, non-conceptual information does not reach the level of conscious processes:

> Such states [i.e., informational states] are not ipso facto perceptual experiences – that is, states of a conscious subject. However addicted we may be to thinking of the links between auditory input and behavioural output in information-processing terms – in terms of computing the solution to simultaneous equations – it seems abundantly clear that evolution could throw up an organism in which such advantageous links were established, long before it had provided us with a conscious subject of experience (Evans, 1982, p. 158).

---

[9] The same description can also be applied to other sensory modalities.

It turns out that non-conceptual content does not provide a satisfactory account of conscious experience. The constraint on non-conceptual content as the representational content of sub-personal processes is due to Evans' 'Kantian conception' of experience, according to which a conscious experience cannot exist without the subjects being self-conscious and objectively aware of things in the world. Therefore, from this point of view, non-conceptual content per se cannot provide the kind of information that allows a subject to have an objective experience of objects. In fact:

> An adequate Idea of an object involves either a conception of it as the occupant of such-an-such a position (at such-and-such time), or a knowledge of what it is for an object so identified to be the relevant object (or, equivalently, what it is for the relevant object to be at a particular position in space and time). (Evans, 1982, p. 149).

By possessing a concept (or Idea) of an object, a subject is, thus, able to identify that specific object, and, as required by the Generality Constraint, entertain an indefinite number of related thoughts about it. Now, the process of locating objects requires the construction of an objective and complete representation of the surrounding in which the spatial relations between objects are specified. In order to achieve this it is necessary to incorporate non-conceptual information with conceptual elements:

> [...] We arrive at conscious perceptual experience when sensory input is not only connected to behavioural dispositions in the way I have been describing – perhaps in some phylogenetically more ancient part of the brain – but also serves as the input to a *thinking, concept-applying, and reasoning system*; so that the subject's thoughts, plans, and deliberations are also systematically dependent on the informational properties of the input. When there is such a further link, we can say that the person, rather than just some part of his brain, receives and possesses information (Evans, 1982, p. 158).

Thus, experiencing the world is a rational process grounded into the external world through non-conceptual information. At the same time, judgments about our experience are not judgments about the content of non-conceptual representations: Non-conceptual information causes higher-level processes but does not fully determine the content of conceptual representations. Rather, the information-link between cognitive and sensory processes is necessary to ground experience in the world, so that the rational processes of judging, thinking, and believing are satisfied if and only if the contents of our judgments, thoughts, and beliefs match the actual state of the world.

The role of the representation of object locations to properly identify objects is also considered by Peacocke (1992b). He argues that the representation of, so-called, scenario contents is necessary to recognize objects. A scenario content is defined by two conditions: *(i)* The ability to represent object locations; and *(ii)* the individuation of the object features at each location in space. The location of objects in a scenario content is in egocentric coordinates: The origin and the axes of this coordinate system are posited on the subject's body – the origin is represented by the center of the chest and the axes represent the three cardinal directions: up/down, left/right, and back/front. Once the axes are defined, the scenario content individuates the properties that fill each point in the represented space. Hence, the scenario content individuates the ways of filling out the space around the perceiver. For example, the experience of a green balloon on the subject's right side depends on the information about both the balloon being on the right position relative to the subject's body and its being green, round, with a certain brightness, texture, etc. The content of experience is correct if the perceived scene falls under the way of locating surfaces and the other properties constituting the scenario, so that the experience of the green balloon is true if and only if the content of the scenario representing green and round patches at a specific location matches the position of the green balloon in the external world.

Scenario content is necessary to capture the content of a visual experience, though it is not necessary. A full description of a visual experience involves an additional source of information to describe the relation among an object's parts and between different objects (e.g., 'X is parallel to Y', 'H is symmetrical about Z', and so on). This information – *protopropositional content* (Peacocke, 1992b) – is necessary to properly identify objects. Protopropositional contents are not determined by scenario contents. In fact, we can experience scenarios with the same properties but with different protopropositional descriptions. For example, the representations of structurally related objects, such as, for example, a diamond and a square, have common scenario contents that represent the same sides, colors, and so on. Nevertheless, the geometrical relations among their sides distinguish a diamond from a square: "When something is perceived as a diamond, the perceived symmetry is a symmetry about the bisectors of its angles. When something is perceived as a square, the perceived symmetry is a symmetry about the bisector of its side (Peacocke, 1992b, p. 119)." Information about symmetry and other spatial relations is carried by the protopropositional content. Thus, the protopropositional content carries higher-level information (i.e., spatial relations) as opposed to the scenario content that carries primitive sensory information (i.e., object locations and feature values). The combination of information represented by scenario and protopropositional contents results in the complete representation of the content of a visual scene.

The description of the scenario content as a way of filling out the space around the perceiver recalls the empirical notion of topographic *feature maps* (Treisman, 1993). Feature maps are retinotopically organized visual cortical areas, each of which represents a specific feature value occurring at different locations within the visual field. An influential hypothesis considers the representation of the location at which features occur to play a fundamental role in the visual representation of coherent objects (Treisman, 1988). This hypothesis can be described as a way to represent visual scenes by representing the features that fill in a specific spatial type, as I will describe in chapter four. On the contrary, I do not think that there is something similar to protopropositional content in vision. I will argue that the representation of spatial relations among an object's parts and between objects in a visual scene might be implicitly represented by the visual system. That is to say, vision might only represent where objects' parts and entire objects are located but might not explicitly represent spatial relations among parts and among objects.

1.4 Vision as a Representational System

Teleological approaches to the study of representations (Millikan, 1984; Drestke, 1995) provide an explanation of how the content of visual experience is acquired by considering the properties that a representational system, *qua* representational, should exhibit.

A system is representational if it has the function to encode specific properties. For example, the function of a clock is to provide information about time: Whenever the clock's hands position changes, the clock provides information about the passing of units of time. Because it has the function to encode information about temporal changes, the clock, by definition, represents time. The same definition applies to sensory organs: A sensory organ represents specific properties of the world because its biological function is to extract and carry information about those properties.[10] Thus, the content of experience is determined by the biological function of the sensory system of which it is the state, and its content is satisfied if the sensory system correctly represents the state of affairs corresponding to the actual state of affair in the world. Teleological accounts of representation content seem to involve fully predetermined and not fallible representational processes. Nevertheless, misrepresentation can occur. Consider, again, the example of the clock: If, for example, the clock has not been charged up for a long time, then it would stop to correctly represent the time, namely, it would misrepresent time.

The definition of misrepresentation is necessary to refine the notion of representation: Only if a system has the function to represent certain information it can misrepresent them. Misrepresentation is phenomenally perceived at the level of conscious experience, and, at the same time, indicates an alteration of the sensory processes that causes the erroneous representation.

Let us consider if and how misrepresentation can occur during visual information processing. Roughly, the visual system is composed of several specialized

---

[10] Dretske (1995) distinguishes between natural and conventional representations. Natural representations result from the activity of systems that are biologically determined for a specific function. That is, their biological function depends on their evolutionary history. Conventional representations, instead, result form the activity of artificial systems. That is, systems that are designed for having specific informational functions such as, for example, a thermometer.

components: Cones and rods for extracting visual information under different light conditions (daylight or night) and colors, clusters of neurons that respond to particular features (color, orientation, motion directions, etc.), specific pathways for information about object identity ('what') and object location ('where'), etc. Each of these components has the biological function to carry specific information about the world. But is vision a representational system, too? If we can account for misrepresentation in vision, then sub-conscious visual processing involves operations on representations with a non-conceptual content. Plausible examples of visual misrepresentations are visual afterimages: These are the illusory percepts evoked by stabilizing our gaze on an image and, then, suddenly viewing a surface of uniform luminance and color. A common afterimage results from staring for a few seconds at a dark line against a bright background, and, by moving the gaze to a darker surface, one illusory experiences a bright line against the dark surface. This 'misperception' is explained by mechanisms of sensory adaptation: In the original image, the part of the retina on which the dark line is projected is not activated; the rest of the retina is strongly activated by the bright background. As a consequence, the photoreceptors on that part of the retina are adapted: Neurons that fire for the bright background adapt (or fatigue), namely, those neurons either they stop firing or lower their activations. After adaptation, the unadapted photoreceptors (i. e., neurons that code for the dark line) become more active than the adapted ones, which, in turn, give rise to the illusory percept of a bright line against a dark background. Visual afterimages seem to be a case of misrepresentation: The photoreceptors have the proper function to carry information about contrast and light condition but if their activity is altered, as, for example, during adaptation, then the activity of photoreceptors gives rise to an illusory/wrong representation of the contrast and light information that they carry.

Besides the possibility of misrepresentation, informational states have to satisfy two additional criteria in order to be conceived as representational (Bermúdez, 1995, p. 349): *(i)* They should admit of cognitive integration; and *(ii)* they should be compositionally structured in such a way that their elements can be constituents of other representational states.

Cognitive integration depends on the storage of previously processed representations. The matching between a perceived novel representation and a previously stored one is necessary to allow a fast and flexible recognition ability that identifies novel representations as tokens of the same types of stored representations. Cognitive integration is involved in different processes, such as, for example, propositional attitude processes and object recognition. For example, structural models of visual object recognition distinguish among different processes within the visual system, each of which represents different features of increasing complexities (Marr, 1982; Biederman, 1987). The final output of these initial processes, i. e., an object representation, has to match some object templates stored in visual memory in order to recognize the represented object, and, thus, the recognition process to end. Structural models of object recognition provide, thus, evidence for cognitive integration to occur in vision.

The argument for the compositionality of informational systems involves structured representations. In Evans' view, only thought is a structured representational system. Particularly, thoughts are structured in a systematic way, so that if a subject is able to think 'Fa' and 'Gb', she is also able to think 'Fb' and 'Ga'. The ability to entertain systematic related thoughts is one of the characteristic features of thought, as described by the Generality Constraint. The Generality Constraint and the argument for the systematicity of thought (Fodor and Pylyshyn, 1988) refer to a similar ability, namely, the ability to entertain structurally related thoughts. However, systematicity is normally considered to be a general property of mental representations, as opposed to the Generality Constraint that specifies an intrinsic feature of thought. The relation between the Generality Constraint and systematicity is as follows: A subject's thoughts are systematic only if a subject satisfies the Generality Constraint in respect to them. Notice that, notwithstanding the similarity between the Generality Constraint and systematicity, Evans does not commit himself to the view of language-like processes that underlie thought production, as the account of systematicity in the Language of Thought theory (Fodor, 1998a). Nevertheless, I will consider systematicity as a good implementation of the Generality Constraint in mental processes, and consider what are the requirements a system has to satisfy in order to be systematic, or, in other words, to satisfy the Generality Constraint.

According to the Generality Constraint and the argument for the systematicity of thought, systematicity is a pervasive property of higher-cognitive systems. Vision as a non-conceptual sensory process, instead, is not systematic. Since systematicity involves compositionality, if informational processes are not systematic, then they also fail to be compositional. I think that before ruling out vision as a structured system, it is necessary to investigate which are the properties of the structure of visual processes, as described by findings in vision science, in order to evaluate whether vision has a systematic and compositional structure of constituents.

1.5 Conclusion

This chapter describes vision as a representational system with non-conceptual mental representations. Because of its particular structure and content, vision does not seem to share properties with higher-level cognitive systems. For example, Evans considers the representational character to be the only common feature that these systems share. On the contrary, I will argue in the next chapters that operations in the visual system display some further properties that are normally considered as constitutive of conceptual processes. I will focus, in particular, on the systematicity and compositionality of vision. As I said before, the analysis of these features requires a complete understanding of the mode of processing of visual representations. However, before considering it, I will describe in the next chapter what are the requirements that a system that has a systematic and compositional structure of constituents has to meet.

2
Syntactic Compositionality, Systematicity, and Productivity

It has been argued that the first occurrence of the principle of semantic compositionality can be traced back to Frege (1892). It is still a matter of discussion, which role the principle of semantic compositionality had in his philosophy (Pelletier, 2001), but it plays a predominant role in contemporary semantics. Compositionality specifies how the meaning of a complex expression depends on the meaning of other expressions that are part of it. Specifically, the principle of semantic compositionality is defined as follows:

[C] The meaning of a complex sentence is function of the meaning of its components and the way they combine.

There are different interpretations of [C] depending on how its terms are defined (Pelletier, 1994; Janssen, 1997). However, what matters is that all the possible interpretations of the principle of semantic compositionality share some assumptions about the main properties of cognitive systems.

Compositionality is a property of natural language and thought. According to a particular interpretation of the principle of compositionality, the relation between language and thought is as such that sentences in a natural language express thoughts, so that the content of a language sentence is the content of the thought it expresses. Hence, the compositionality of natural language is a manifestation of the compositionality of thought (Evans, 1982; Fodor, 2001). The principle of compositionality of thought describes how the content of a complex thought depends on the content of primitive mental representations and how structured mental representations are combined during thought processing.[1] In this work, I mainly focus on the principle of compositionality of thought, since it specifies the content of mental representations.

If a system is compositional, then the following other properties apply (Fodor, 1998a): *(i)* It has a structure of constituents; *(ii)* it is systematic; and *(iii)* it is productive. The structure of constituents refers to the fact that a thought is constructed out of building blocks. For example, the thought 'John loves Mary' is built up by combining the representations 'John', 'Loves', and 'Mary'. Systematicity relates to the fact that the ability to entertain certain thoughts is related to the ability to entertain other related thoughts. The classical example for systematicity is that it is difficult to find someone that can think John loves the girl but cannot think the

---

[1] I assume, for present purposes, that the meaning of a word in a sentence expresses the content of a concept in thought. I will, thus, indiscriminately use content and meaning.

girl loves John (Fodor and Pylyhsyn, 1988). Productivity refers to the creative side of thought: It refers to the ability to think an indefinite number of thoughts, even if the thought system has access to a limited representational resource. Notice that compositionality alone is not sufficient to guarantee productivity. It is necessary to appeal to the distinction between competence and performance (Chomsky, 1965). Competence is an abstract property of cognitive systems that involves the ability to understand and produce indefinitely many sentences and thoughts (Fodor and Pylyshyn, 1988), by postulating an abstract recursive mechanism that allows indefinite recombinations of constituents from a finite set of primitives. Instead, performance is the actual finite ability to produce thoughts. A cognitive system is productive if it implements the recursive mechanisms underlying the abstract competence. Whether the thought system is productive is a matter of discussion (Fodor and Pylyshyn, 1988). However, it has been argued that, even if a system does not allow for indefinite productive processes (i. e., if a system is a finite computational system), systematicity still holds as a property of systems with compositional structures of constituents (Fodor, 2001). This last statement is important for the analysis of the properties of visual structured processes, since vision, as I will argue, is not productive, and yet is systematic and compositional. To this extent, I hypothesize that it is possible to apply the principles of the theory of compositionality of thought to the description of processes involved in visual object representation. This is because visual object representation involves operations on structured representations.

In order to describe the compositionality and systematicity of visual object representation, it is necessary to reconsider some of the consequences of the principle of semantic compositionality. Specifically, I will propose a principle of compositionality – syntactic compositionality – that is similar to *deflationary* accounts of the role of compositionality in determining theories of meaning (Horwich, 1997, 2001, 2005). The rest of the chapter will focus on the definition of the principle of syntactic compositionality, the description of systematicity, and why productivity is not a property of visual processes. A more detailed description of how vision coherently represents objects, and the systematicity and compositionality of object representation will follow in the next chapters.

2.1 Varieties of Compositionality

There are so many theories of compositionality that one can easily loose one's way in trying to understand what exactly compositionality involves (see, for example, Szabó, 2000). I will simplify matters by focusing only on those aspects that are necessary for defining the compositionality of structured visual processes. In order to do that, I will first introduce one of the most complete accounts of compositionality of mental processes – Fodor's theory of compositionality –, and, immediately after, I will evaluate reasons for believing that this kind of compositionality is too strong a principle for explaining cognitive processes.

2.1.1 *The principle of compositionality of thought*

Fodor's account of compositionality is part of his attempt to give a naturalized explanation of propositional attitudes. A propositional attitude is a mental state described by the following expression: X believes/hopes/wishes/ … that P, where P is a proposition that expresses the object of the belief, hope, wish, and so on. The belief that John Loves Mary is an example of a propositional attitude. A subject's being in a propositional attitude state consists in the subject's bearing a functional/computational relation to a mental representation:

For any organism O, and any attitude A toward the proposition P, there is a ('computational'/'functional') relation R and a mental representation MP such that MP means that P, and O has A iff O bears R to MP. (Fodor, 1987, p. 17).

It is often referred to Fodor's theory of mental processes as the Language of Thought Theory (LOT), since it postulates a system of mental representations with a compositional syntax and semantics (Fodor, 1975). A compositional syntax requires a system of atomic mental representations, so that complex mental representations are built up from the syntactic combination of primitive representations. For example, the thought $P \wedge Q$[2] derives its structure from combining the primitive representations for P and Q through conjunction. Operations on primitive representations are sensitive to their structures: Processes in LOT transform a representation that satisfies a particular syntactic structure into a representation that satisfies another syntactic structure. For example, in the case of inference, an architecture based on LOT transforms the input representation $(P \wedge Q) \wedge Z$, and given $(P \wedge Q)$, into the output representation Z. On top of that, LOT has a compositional semantics: The content of a complex representation like $P \wedge Q$ depends on the content of its components; namely, it depends on the content of the mental representations P and Q. The principle of compositionality of thought can be defined as follows:

[CT] The content of a thought (i.e., a complex mental representation) is determined by the content of its constituents and its syntactic structure.

[CT] is a stronger version of the principle of compositionality than the one presented in [C]. It requires the content of a thought to be actually determined by its parts: The content of the thought that P is determined only if its constituents $\langle p_1, …, p_n \rangle$ are explicitly tokened. This directly follows from the fact that

---

[2] Mental representation in Fodor's theory is synonyms of thought (Fodor, 1998a). Thus, thoughts, as mental representations, express the object of propositional attitudes.

processes in LOT are causally sensitive to the structure of primitive representations: It is not possible to entertain a complex thought like 'John loves Mary' if the
primitive representations on which the processes apply are not explicitly tokened.

The principle of compositionality, as stated in [CT], turns to be a ruling
principle in defining the elementary properties that determine the content of the
constituents. In fact, the content of a complex thought depends not only on the
meaning of its constituents, but also the constituents have to contribute with *all*
their content to the content of the whole (Fodor, 2001). Thus, [CT] constrains
theories of concept[3] possession, since not all the properties that constitute the
content of a primitive constituents compose (Fodor, 1998b). It follows that the
properties that determine the content of the constituents have to be included
as properties of the content of a complex thought. Hence, if the possession of
a primitive concept depends on its content being determined, for example, by
some G-properties, then G-properties are part of the content of the complex
thought in which the primitive concepts are tokened (see Horwich, 2001). For
example, if a theory of concept possession requires that having a concept depends
on epistemic properties like recognitional capacities, being a prototype, etc., then,
according to the principle of compositionality, as defined in [CT], the content of
a complex thought will show those epistemic properties as well. That is to say,
its content will depend on recognitional and prototypical properties. To take a
further example: If having the concept RED depends on the ability to recognize
good instances of red things and if having the concept SQUARE requires the
ability to recognize good instances of square things, then the possession of the
complex concept RED SQUARE will depend on the ability to recognize good
instances of red-square things. Fodor (1998b, ch. 4 and 5; 2001) argues that this
is not the case, since recognitional capacities, and in general epistemic properties,
do not compose. It is conceivable to possess the concept RED SQUARE, and
at the same time to lack the ability to recognize general instances of the concept
RED. This contradicts the requirement of [CT] – the content of a complex
expression depends on the content of its constituents – since if the content of
the constituents is determined by recognitional capacities, then the content of the
complex thought has to be determined by those properties as well. Thus, the
principle of compositionality rules out some of the theories of content possession.
However, Fodor does not seem to have a better account of how the content
of primitive constituents might be acquired. He proposes a theory based on
informational semantics – asymmetric dependence theory (Fodor, 1987) – that
faces serious problems.[4] Here, my interest is not in whether such a theory offers a
solution for problems in theories of concepts possession. Rather, my interest is on

---

[3] Concepts, *qua* mental representations, are the constituents of thoughts.

[4] See Loewer and Rey (1991) for criticisms on Fodor's asymmetric dependence theory and his reply
to them.

whether [CT] can satisfy an account of the compositionality of mental processes other than thought.

There are reasons to consider [CT] as too a strong requirement for also explaining the compositionality of thought. It has been argued that the semantic requirement of compositionality is not necessary to account for the content of thoughts (see, for example, Schiffer, 1991). Specifically, the principle of compositionality can be reformulated only in syntactic terms, in which the content of primitive constituents plays only a secondary role in the determination of the content of the final representation. A main argument to take into account in the definition of a syntactic theory of compositionality is based on the assumption that the principle of compositionality does not impose constraints on theories of content for either complex representations or primitive representations.

2.1.2 *Compositionality deflated*

The deflationary theory of compositionality lessens the role of [CT] in determining the content of primitive constituents (Horwich, 1997, 2001, 2005). The main idea is that compositionality *per se* does not impose any constraints on how the meaning of words is constituted. Thus, according to the deflationary account, it is not a problem if, for example, epistemic properties do not compose, since:

> The property that is responsible for a *complex's* meaning what it does *isn't* a use or inferential role, *isn't* a stereotype or prototype, and *isn't* a recognitional capacity, but is rather the property of being constructed in a certain way from words with certain uses, or associated prototypes, or recognitional capacities, ..., or whatever other characteristics one takes to engender the meanings of words. (Horwich, 2005, p. 217, *italics PH*).

The aim of a deflationary account of compositionality is to constrain the role of compositionality in determining the meaning of the primitive constituents in natural language sentences. But this approach can also be applied to the content of thought constituents, if one considers, as I already observed, the content of a language expression to express the content of a thought. On top of that, the deflationary approach also rules out the role of combinatorial semantics in determining the meaning of a complex sentence. The meaning of a complex expression results from imposing a particular structure to words independently of whatever properties a theory of meaning attributes to the components. Specifically, the meaning of a complex expression reduces to its construction properties; so that it results from combining words with particular meanings according to a particular structure (Horwich, 1997). Thus, for example, the sentence 'John loves Mary' has that particular meaning because a structure of the kind ⟨Subject, Verb, Object⟩ is applied to the words 'John', 'Loves', 'Mary'. The deflated principle of compositionality can be defined as follows:

[CD] The content of a complex expression depends on the structure imposed on its constituents that have a particular meaning.

[CD] makes easier to see why compositionality holds, since the determination of the meaning of a complex expression reduces mainly to how the primitive elements are combined. In fact, if the meaning of a sentence depends on the role of the constituents in the sentence, then its meaning does not need to share all the properties that engender the meanings of the constituents.

2.1.3 *Syntactic compositionality*

The deflationary approach to compositionality defines the content of a complex expression (representation) as being mainly determined by the way its constituents are combined. Therefore, the determination of the content of the constituents becomes independent of the principle of compositionality. Nevertheless, [CD] is an attempt to explain how conceptual content composes. That is to say, Horwich's deflationary account defines how sentences (thoughts) have a particular content by claiming that the content of a whole depends on the structural relations among conceptual primitive constituents. Instead, I need a definition of the principle of compositionality that elucidates how the content of non-conceptual representations is derived by the structural processes that combine together primitive non-conceptual constituents. The definition of a principle of compositionality of non-conceptual representations is necessary insofar as one considers vision as a structured system with operations on a set of primitive non-conceptual representations. The principle of syntactic compositionality is defined as follows:

[CS] The content of a non-conceptual complex representation depends on the structure imposed on its constituents that have a specific content.

If one's interest is to explain how we master language, then it is quite likely that the structure one recognizes as being imposed on constituents tend to have the form of the grammar for a particular language (see, for example, Horwich, 2005). For example, the content of the expression 'John dances' is given by applying the structure ⟨S V⟩ in English to words that have the meaning JOHN and DANCES. Whether this structure applies to all the known languages is a matter of debate in linguistics. Nevertheless, the same structure applies to artificial languages, like the one, for example, postulated by LOT theory. In fact, the content of the thought $P \wedge Q$ is determined by applying the rule for conjunction to the constituents P and Q. The variety of syntactic operations to be applied to a set of representations in artificial and natural languages is larger than the ones so far presented. However, the essence of the argument stays the same if we consider all the possible combinations of operations on constituents allowed in LOT.

Nevertheless, I doubt that the kind of operations on inner mental representations posited by the Language of Thought theory defines a standard set of operations that is valid for mental processes other than thought. I hypothesize that a system could share some properties with the thought system with a restricted number of, or without, the same kind of operations on primitive representations. Particularly, vision seems to be that kind of system. What I want to show is that visual object representation is a compositional, and systematic process, even if its structure diverges from the one postulated in LOT theory. I argue that operations in visual object representation mostly reduce to conjunction and identity. These are necessary operations to combine visual primitive representations and represent coherent objects. For the moment, we can disregard the details of the visual processing of object representations, and focus on how the principle of compositionality as defined in [CS] describes the compositionality of vision.

According to [CS], the content of a complex representation depends on the structure imposed on its primitive representations. Thus, I need to show whether, and how, the content of a visual object representation depends on its constituents. In formal terms, the operations that underlie visual object representation can be described by a language V with the following primitive vocabulary: A finite set of primitive visual representations $\langle v_1, \ldots, v_n \rangle$ and the operations $\langle \wedge, = \rangle$ (Clark, 2000; Werning, 2005). Hence, the visual representation of, for example, 'Red Square and Green Triangle' can be formalized in this way:

Let be $\langle v_1, v_2, v_3, v_4 \rangle v_1$ the set of primitive representations for Red (v_1), Square (v_2), Green (v_3), and Triangle (v_4); then:

(∗) $(v_1 \wedge v_2 \wedge v_3 \wedge v_4)$

represents the visual representation (Red and Square and Green and Triangle).

However, conjunction alone is not sufficient to link together the attributes that belong to the same object: The conjunction of primitive representations in (∗) allows different combinations of the constituents, so that (∗) can be recombined to represent 'Green Square and Red Triangle'. In order to fix the attributes that belong to the representation of a particular object, processes in visual object representation lock the visual primitive representations to a particular entity, so that visual primitive representations play the role of predicates. This is necessary to secure the identity of an object. How the visual system properly attributes visual features to the right object is known in vision science as the *binding problem* (Hardcastle, 1994). Different explanations of the binding problem have been provided but the main hypotheses are: (*i*) Features are bound according to the location where they occur (Treisman and Gelade, 1980; Clark, 2004a); and (*ii*) features are bound to objects (Pylyshyn, 2007, Cohen, 2004a). Notwithstanding the differences between the location-based and the object-based accounts of binding, the solutions to the binding problem describe visual object representation as having the following form:

$$(**)\qquad (v_1(x) \wedge v_2(x)) \wedge (v_3(y) \wedge v_4(y))$$

Where x represents the region of space or object to which the attributes Red and Square belong to; and y represents the region of space or object to which the attributes Green and Triangle belong. How $(**)$ is implemented in the visual system, and if this process actually involves the tokening of primitive constituents is a matter of study in the subsequent chapters.

As opposed to [CT], the principle of syntactic compositionality does not commit to provide a theory of how the meaning of primitive constituents is acquired, and neither it does the deflationary account of compositionality [CD]. Because of lacking a theory of lexical meaning, it has been argued that [CD] is a vacuous account of compositionality.[5] The same does not apply to the principle of syntactic compositionality, since it defines how the content of non-conceptual representations composes. Hence, there is no need to refer to a theory of lexical meaning to determine the content of the constituents.

The content of visual representations is non-conceptual. That is, a subject does not need to possess the concepts required to describe a visual scene. One can lack the concepts RED and APPLE and yet perceive a red apple. The content of non-conceptual mental representations can be described in a naturalistic way through the notion of teleological function, that is, of the extrinsic property of a system. Thus, the content of a mental representation is defined according to what information a particular system is wired to carry. The visual system, with its specialized neuronal maps and paths, is a good example of a system that represents the world because its subsystems have the biological function to react only to specific information. Hence, to explain the compositionality of vision one does not need to explain either how a subject acquires a concept or why a primitive representation has certain content.

The compositionality of vision turns to have the following form: The composition of the content of an object's visual representation depends on the way the visual primitive representations are combined. The content carried by visual representations plays a role in determining the content of the object representation but in a way that it is more similar to Horwich's deflationary view than to the strong Fodorian requirement.

---

[5] See Horwich (1997) for a detailed description of criticisms of [CD].

2.2 Structure of Constituents

For a system to be compositional, it has to implement a particular structure: The structure of constituents. A constituent is an entity, in every primitive process, that corresponds to the smallest meaningful representation carrying relevant information for the processing of more complex representations. There is no univocal theory of what a constituent is. One finds, instead, if one considers theories of mental processes, at least two different interpretations of the nature of constituents:

1) Constituents are concepts (Fodor, 1998a): The definition of constituents as primitive concepts non-further decomposable is part of LOT theory. In this framework, the constituents of the thought aRb are the primitive concepts $\underline{a}$, $\underline{b}$ and the double-place relation R that indicates a concept as well. To take the same example, the constituents of the thought 'John loves Mary' are the primitive concepts JOHN, LOVE, and MARY that correspond to primitive mental representations that cannot be further decomposed and are identified by their structure and their content (Fig. 2.1a).

2) Constituents are sub-symbols (Smolensky, 1988): The story is different if one considers the nature of primitive representations from a connectionist point of view; particularly, if one considers connectionist models that simulate language-like structures (see, for example, Smolensky, 1990, 1991). The primitive constituents of thought processes are sub-symbols: Primitive representations that are finer-grained than the symbols used at the conceptual level of language explanation. Thus, for example, the constituents of an expression like 'John loves Mary' are activity vectors over individual units, which represent microfeatures (sub-symbols). Constituents in a neural network can be combined either by vectorial sums or by a combination of primitive vectorial operations and role vectors (i.e., Tensor product; Smolensky, 1990). For example, the representation of 'John loves Mary' in a connectionist neural network is in, the case of vectorial sum, $\{$ *John-subject* + *Mary-object* + *Loves-verb* $\}$; and, in the case of tensor operations, $\{$ *John* $\otimes$ *subject* + *Mary* $\otimes$ *object* + *Loves* $\otimes$ *verb* $\}$ or for a further decomposition: $(\{ J \otimes 1 + O \otimes 2 + H \otimes 3 + N \otimes 4 \} + \{ M \otimes 1 + A \otimes 2 + R \otimes 3 + Y \otimes 4 \} + \{ L \otimes 1 + O \otimes 2 + V \otimes 3 + E \otimes 4 + S \otimes 5 \})$, where $\otimes$ represents the multiplication of vectors or tensor product (Fig. 2.1b). Primitive constituents correspond to the activity of the units in the network. Particularly, each constituent is made of the activity of groups of units that become active whenever the information they code for is given as an input to the network. Hence, units that code for a specific features are active whenever that feature is present. For this reason, different representations, such as for example, the representations of John and Mary might be given by the distributed activation of some overlapping units (Hinton *et al.*, 1986).

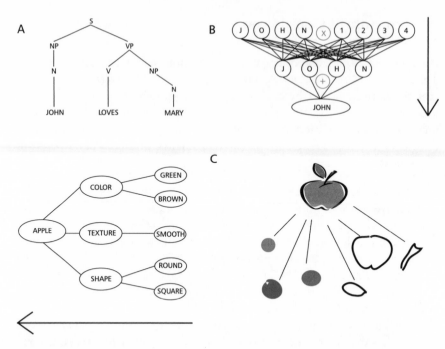

Fig. 2.1: Structure of constituents: (A) represents the decomposition of a complex expression in LOT; (B) shows how a neural network builds up a complex representation of language expression; and (C) represents how a visual scene is decomposed according to the Perceptual Symbol System hypothesis (right), and its relation to frame theories of language categorization (left).

The distributed structure of artificial neural networks resembles the structure of the visual system. In fact, vision is a highly parallel and hierarchical system, in which information is processed in distinct areas and increases in complexity at the highest-level of the hierarchy. Evidence from psychophysical and neuroscientific studies supports the idea that the representation of visual scenes is processed in several distinct areas, each of which is specific for particular information. A theoretical model of the constituent structure of visual object representation is Barsalou's Perceptual Symbol System (Barsalou, 1999; Fig. 2.1c). Barsalou argues that a mechanism based on *frames* composed of visual symbolic representations can be the basis of object categorization in vision (Barsalou, 1999; Barsalou *et al.*, 2003). A *frame* can be considered as a broad category that can be further decomposed in related concepts (Barsalou, 1992). For example, the concept APPLE can be decomposed into its constituent concepts: COLOR, TEXTURE, SHAPE, etc. At the same time, each part can be further decomposed in more elementary constituents like, for example, GREEN, BROWN, SMOOTH, and ROUND. The main difference with LOT theory is that none of the concepts represented in the frame is a primitive concept. In fact, each primitive concept can be a complex concept and further decomposed into more primitive constituents. The process of decomposition goes, in principle, indefinitely (Barsalou, 1992, p. 41).

The hypothesis of a perceptual symbol system with a distributed structure of constituents integrates evidence from vision science with distributed models of neural representation. However, this hypothesis focuses on the explanation of visual categorization, by considering visual primitive representations as conceptual representations combined according to formal rules. Instead, I want to argue that a similar distributed structure of constituents is involved in non-conceptual visual processes prior to object categorization. This will make a difference also in the kinds of operations that allow the combination of visual constituents.

Postulating one kind of constituents rather than another is orthogonal to the fact that a system is compositional, systematic, and productive. The principle of compositionality and its related features hold independently of the kind of constituents involved. Rather, it is the relation that holds between an expression and its constituents that defines the basic structure for a compositional, systematic, and productive system. The relation of constituency is defined as a mereological relation, namely, as a relation of parts to whole (Fodor and McLaughlin, 1990; Fodor, 1996): Every time the expression E is tokened, its constituents $\langle e_1, \ldots, e_n \rangle$ are tokened, too.

The relation of constituency constrains the kind of architecture that can explain compositional processes, since constituents need to have a causal role in the construction of the output representation. Classical architectures based on LOT account for how cognitive processes can encode such a relation, since the roles of symbols in a propositional process are defined according to their positions in the tokened expression. Instead, it is problematic to account for the relation of constituency in neural networks, mainly because constituents in connectionist networks seem to not play a causal role in the building up of a representation. It has been argued that if a cognitive model fails to implement the constituency relation, then it cannot explain the systematicity of cognitive systems (Fodor and McLaughlin, 1990; Fodor, 1996).

2.3 Systematicity

The structure of constituents is a pre-requisite for explaining the systematic behavior of thought production. Systematicity refers to the ability to entertain structural related thoughts: If a subject is able to think *aRb*, she is also able to think *bRa* (Fodor and Pylyshyn, 1988).

In a classical account of thought processes, systematicity results from processes that are sensitive to the structure of constituents: The ability to entertain related thoughts depends on the fact that different combinations of constituents have the same syntactic structure. To take an example, the thoughts 'John loves Mary' and 'Mary loves John' share the same structure ⟨S V O⟩, even if the constituents that occupy the *slots* ⟨S V O⟩ are different. Thus, systematicity is a lawful relation between certain abilities that is explained by appeal to a syntactic property of processes on inner mental representations (McLaughlin, 2009).

Systematicity and compositionality are closely related. On the one hand, a different combination of the same constituents brings to a different content of a complex expression. On the other hand, the principle of compositionality posits that the content of the constituents remains identical even if the structure changes.

Systematicity holds also in the framework of [CS] because systematicity is explained by referring to a syntactic property of systems with a structure of constituents. [CS] determines the content of a complex expression primarily considering the role of syntactic combinations of constituents. As an extent, it can be argued that the principle of compositionality in [CS] is nothing over and above systematicity, since the determination of the content of a complex expression relies completely on structural operations on primitive representations. However, this is not the case: Even if [CS] focuses particularly on syntactic properties, rather than defining constraints on the content of primitive representations, the content of the constituents plays an important role in the definition of the content of a complex representation. For this reason, systematicity does not reduce to [CS]. Rather, it is an empirical property of a system that has a compositional structure of constituents, as defined among others by [CS].

My aim is to evaluate whether vision is a systematic system. The first hint for explaining systematicity in different cognitive modalities is supported by the hypothesis that systematicity is a pervasive feature of human and non-human cognition (Fodor and Pylyshyn, 1988). The argument goes like this: It is hard to imagine that humans and animals are capable to entertain only a finite number of unrelated thoughts, so that an animal can learn to react to the stimulus *aRb* but it cannot represent the state of affair *bRa*. 'To react to a stimulus' means that an animal is able to behave according to what is represented in a scene. This representation includes the representation of a visual scene *as* having that particular content. Representing something *as* involves conceptual abilities. Thus, the explanation of the systematic ability of non-human animals is still given in a conceptual framework: The capacity to represent the state of affair *aRb* and *bRa* is expressed by the conceptual ability of, for example, *seeing* something *as aRb* or *as bRa*. Note that 'seeing as' and 'thinking that' are both intentional states in the same intentional mode (McLaughlin, 1993a).[6]

---

[6] Whether animals (and humans) have systematic conceptual abilities has been matter of discussion. For example, Andy Clark (1991) argues against systematicity of thought, and defends a systematicity of behavior for animals (see, also, McLaughlin, 1993b, for a reply to Clark's criticisms).

In order to consider the systematicity of vision in a way that rules out the conceptual influence of language and thought, it is necessary to evaluate whether structural related visual scenes represent a recombination of the same constituents. An example of systematic process in visual object representation, similar to what presented so far, is the ability to see a Square Above a Triangle (*aRb*) and a Triangle Above a Square (*bRa*). It might seem trivial to explain systematicity for vision, since it is obvious that one can perceive the combination of objects thereof. However, the processes involved in the representation of those scenes turn to be less than trivial once we focus on how the visual system represents *aRb* and *bRa*.

2.3.1 *The binding problem in artificial neural networks*

A major challenge that cognitive models based on artificial neural networks have to face is the explanation of systematicity, and the binding problem related to it (Fodor and McLaughlin, 1990; Smolensky, 1991, McLaughlin, 1993a, 2009; Fodor, 1996; Matthews, 1997; von der Malsburg, 1999). The binding problem refers to the ability to properly integrate primitive representations to represent complex mental representations. This problem arises whenever two or more objects have to be represented simultaneously. Examples of binding problems are the representation of the thought 'John loves Mary' in a conceptual system, and the representation of a visual scene with 'a red triangle on top of a green square' within the visual system. Of course, these representations are systematic only if a subject is able to also represent the structural related representations 'Mary loves John' and 'a green square on top of a red triangle'. Note that, whilst systematicity involves that primitive representations are properly bound, the solution to the binding problem does not involve systematicity: One can properly represent, for example, *aRb* and *aRg* but from this it does not follow that one is also able to represent *bRg* (Fodor, 1998a).[7] For the purpose of this work, I will consider the case in which systematicity and binding are related, as in the case of *aRb* and *bRa*.

The explanation of systematicity and the solution to the binding problem require a causal structure of constituents. Classical accounts of cognitive processes implement such a structure, so that the representation of a complex symbol is constructed by explicitly combining primitive symbols. Instead, parallel and distributed models of cognition fail to implement a proper structure of constituents (Fodor and McLaughlin, 1990). The problem arises because distributed networks fail to bind primitive representations according to their causal roles. For example, the representation of 'John loves Mary' is represented in a classical account as $((John)_{NP} ((loves)_V ((Mary_{NP}))_{VP})_S$, in which the roles of the constituents are

---

[7] The explanation of systematicity is contingent upon empirical verification (Fodor and Pylyshyn, 1988). Even if it is hard to conceive a being with a *punctate* mind, it might still be possible that this being exists.

expressed by their position in the expression. It seems that nothing equivalent applies to parallel-distributed models. The representation of the constituents in neural networks is not bound to their roles, such that the representation, for example, of a visual scene with a red triangle on top of a green square leads to a binding ambiguity of which object is on top and which one is at the bottom. The binding problem in neural networks seems not to be resolved, even by explicitly representing the causal roles of the primitive constituents within the network.[8] This solution requires the implementation of a structure like { +triangle-subject, +on top, +square-object}. The problem with this solution is that one needs to postulate an indefinite number of constituents for each of the possible ways the primitive constituents can be combined. If, for example, the square is on top of the triangle, then the representation above becomes { +square-subject, +on top, +triangle-object}, namely, one needs to posit new representations for each novel recombination. This kind of structure faces the following problems: *(i)* It is not a proper structure of constituents, since it fails to represent the same constituents in different recombination. *(ii)* The number of primitive representations involved in the building up of even simple complex representations far reaches the computational limits of any existing computational devise (including the brain).

The lack of a structure of constituents in neural networks involves the inability of connectionist approaches to explain the systematicity of cognitive processes. For this reason, classical neural networks have often been considered as pure association machines, lacking structured processes (Fodor and Pylyshyn, 1988; Clark, Andy, 1993). Whether this is the case for all distributed models of cognition, and specifically, whether this is the case for models of visual object representation, is matter of argument in chapter four.

2.4 Productivity

Productivity identifies a creative property of cognitive processes: It involves our ability to entertain an indefinite number of thoughts (Fodor, 1998a). For example, one can entertain the thoughts 'John loves Mary and walks on the moon every time Mary walks the dog', and 'Mary walks the dog on the moon only on even days', even if it is hard to imagine that one has ever encountered such situations. Frege expressed the productive aspect of natural language as follows:

> Language has the power to express, with comparatively few means such a profusion of thoughts that no one could possibly command a view of them all. What makes this possible is that a thought has parts out of which it is constructed and that these parts

---

[8] See Fodor and Pylyshyn (1988) for a detailed description.

correspond to parts of sentences, by which they are expressed (Frege, 1914, p. 243, in Pelletier, 2001, p. 107).

The claim that thoughts are productive is explained by reference to both the compositional structure of a system and the human linguistic competence (Chomsky, 1965). Competence is an idealized property that describes the unlimited knowledge that a speaker has of her own language, even if, when a person actually speaks, the idealized competence turns to be the finite and comparably poor actual performance. In computational terms, the implementation of competence requires a devise, such as, for example, a Turing Machine, that can implement recursive operations and, at the same time, extend its memory without changing the intrinsic nature of its architecture (Fodor and Pylyshyn, 1988). The extension of memory capacities is required to store the novel recombinations obtained by applying recursive operations on a set of finite representations. Roughly, recursion defines the process whereby the operations can apply to the non-terminal output of previous operations, in principle indefinitely. For example, by applying recursive operations to the thought 'It is true that Milan is in Italy', it is possible to obtain the thoughts 'it is true that it is true that Milan is in Italy', 'it is true that it is true that it is true that Milan is in Italy' and so on. This example describes a special case of computable recursive function: Iteration. Iteration is a process that defines the value of a specific argument of a function by using its value at a previous argument (Odifreddi, 1999). The n-th iteration for a function f is defined as follows:

$$f^{(0)}(x) = x$$
$$f^{(n+1)}(x) = f\,(f^{(n)}(x))$$

then, if $n = 0$

$$f^{(1)}(x) = f(x)$$

if $n = 1$

$$f^{(2)} = f(f(x))$$

etc.

Productivity entails compositionality (Fodor, 1998a): The only way a thought can be productive is by being compositional, otherwise one cannot explain how a subject can, in principle, entertain an indefinite number of thoughts. However, whether it is necessary that a system that is compositional is also productive is matter of argument (Fodor and Pylyshyn, 1988; Fodor, 1998a). In fact, a cognitive architecture might not be able to implement the recursive processes and extended memory that are necessary to explain productivity. This is the case, for example, of neural network models, and I argue that this is also the case for vision.

Intuitively, one can conceive the visual system as a productive system: It is undeniable that we are able to perceive a large amount of different visual scenes.

The ability to perceive novel scenes makes vision a *mundane creative* process (Barsalou and Prinz, 1997). Mundane creativity refers to our daily ability to produce novel behaviors and cognitions on the basis of our perception. But the issue, here, is not whether a visual representation can be instrumental to productive behavior but whether vision has a structure that allows for productivity within vision itself. As a parallel and distributed system, vision implements a finite architecture that does not account for idealized capacities as competence. That is to say, visual representations are bound to the finite actual performance and do not tend to infinite competence. This constraint is due to physical constraints on the visual system: We can represent rich varieties of visual scenes but these varieties are bound to the physical capacities of the visual system.

Nevertheless, even if the visual system is not productive, one can still investigate whether the visual system has a compositional and systematic structure of constituents. In fact, the explanation of systematicity and compositionality can be detached from the argument for productivity in the analysis of systems that have a finite structure (Fodor and Pylyshyn, 1988).

2.5 Conclusion

Compositionality is a pervasive feature of cognition: It is a property of processes on structured representations in different cognitive modalities. However, the principle of compositionality in [C] and in [CM] exclusively describes compositionality as a property of language and thought. I argued that the visual system is a compositional system. To explain compositionality in visual object representation, it is necessary to reconsider the role of semantic properties in the determination of the content of complex representations. On this basis, I defined the principle of syntactic compositionality –[CS]. [CS] is the ground principle for explaining other compositionality related features in vision: the structure of constituents and systematicity. In the next chapters, I am going to argue that vision is a systematic and a compositional system, by integrating philosophical insights into the properties of combinatorial processes with vision studies of the structure of visual binding operations that lead to object representation.

3

The Binding Problem in Vision

It is necessary to analyze the structure of visual object perception in order to determine whether it is a compositional and systematic process. Almost certainly, a multitude of processes takes place in our brain while a stimulus pattern on the retina leads to the conscious recognition of objects embedded in complex natural scenes. However, this chapter mainly focuses on two basic processes, which arguably underlie *all* visual object representations: (*i*) The extraction of so-called 'elementary visual features' (e.g., color, motion, and basic shape features, such as orientation); and (*ii*) the integration of these visual elementary features into representations of coherent wholes. The necessity for the second process is often referred to as the *binding problem* in vision, and has been a matter of intense debate in cognitive neuroscience for several years (Roskies, 1999). This process is of interest to us for two main reasons: (1) Binding appears to be a low-level visual process that is not influenced by higher cognitive processes, such as language and thought; and (2) it imposes structure onto primitive visual representations. To illustrate the binding process, let us consider, a simple visual scene of a girl picking up an apple from an apple tree. Our visual system seems to decompose the objects of this scene in their elementary features, (color, orientation, motion, etc.), and only later recombines these features to create the representation of the girl, the apples, and the apple tree. How is this accomplished? Even if the example above is a typical case of binding, psychophysical and neurophysiological studies of binding consider even simpler scenes in which there is a controlled number of features, like, for example, a visual scene with green-horizontal and red-vertical bars. This chapter presents results and hypotheses based on this type of research.

Although different types of binding and different mechanisms have been discussed (Humphreys and Riddoch, 2006), I am going to mainly focus on a specific type of binding, namely the integration of features from different dimensions occupying the same location in visual space. For example, in a scene made of a green-horizontal and red-vertical bar, green and horizontal occupy the same location in space since they belong to the same object and so do red and vertical. Most likely, the visual system independently analyzes these features at a particular location and re-integrates them only at a later stage. As we will see, many current models of feature binding postulate an active attentional selection mechanism as being critical (Robertson, 2003). William James (1890) intuitively defined attention as a selective mechanism that makes the selected object more vivid and clear, and causes things that are outside its focus to never enter our experience. James' description of attention is currently defined as covert attention. That is, the act of focusing only on one stimulus, resulting in the process of stimulus related information. Specifically, attention influences the way information is processed by the visual system, probably, by enhancing neuronal activity related to the selected stimulus.

A further influential hypothesis considers the temporal correlation of neuronal activity in the visual system to mediate binding (Singer and Gray, 1995). I will present both attentional and synchrony-based models of binding and possible ways to reconcile them. To this end, one has to consider the general principles underlying the architecture of our visual system.

3.1 General Architecture of the Visual System

Our visual system is both a hierarchically organized and parallel-distributed system (Felleman and Van Essen, 1991). It consists of several dozen distinct specialized cortical areas (Grill-Spector and Malach, 2004; Wandell *et al.*, 2005). Roughly, sensory signals from the retina are processed through these areas in the following way (fig. 3.2): After some processing in the retina, visual signals pass from the output layer of the retina, through the Lateral Geniculate Nucleus (LGN) in the thalamus, to the primary visual cortex (V1). Importantly, this retino-geniculo-cortical pathway consists of two parallel channels: The Magnocellular (M) pathway and the Parvocellular (P) pathway. These channels convey information about fundamentally different aspects of the visual world: Information about motion (M pathway), and form and color (P pathway).

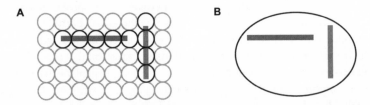

Fig. 3.1: Visual receptive fields (RFs) in different visual areas. (A) RFs of V1 neurons are approximately 2° of the visual field so that these neurons can represent only small parts of the visual stimulus array made up of two bars. (B) RFs of neurons in IT cortex are comparably larger. As a consequence, they typically encompass multiple stimuli of a cluttered visual scene.

The primary visual cortex contains a complete topographic map of the spatial arrangements of the stimuli in the visual field: Each point in V1 corresponds to a point in the retina so that neighboring neurons represent neighboring points in the retina, and the spatial relations among points signaled by photoreceptors in the retina are preserved. The portion of the visual field represented by a neuron is called the neuron's receptive field. The sizes of neurons' receptive fields increase in higher-visual areas, with neurons within V1 having comparably small receptive fields (approximately 2° of the visual field). Thus, individual V1 neurons have access to only a limited subsection of an object represented in the visual field (fig. 3.1).

On top of this spatial selectivity, V1 neurons are also selective for specific features in their receptive fields: Some neurons respond most strongly to specific luminance edge orientations, others are selective for color, or motion direction. When a preferred feature is within a neuron's receptive field, the neuron increases its activity. The activity of a neuron is typically measured by counting the number of spikes during a certain time window (firing rate). The firing rate is close to zero when a neuron is not signaling a stimulus and increases when a preferred stimulus is within the neuron's receptive field. Hence, a neuron's firing rate increases and its signal becomes stronger when a preferred feature is within the neuron's receptive field. Therefore, cortical neurons can be considered as local *feature detectors*. The entire spatial layout of these feature detectors is often described as topographic *feature maps*, made of feature detectors (Julesz, 1981; Treisman, 1993).

V1 projects to a large number of, so-called, extrastriate visual areas. The separation between M and P pathways is being preserved, in that the two corresponding cell groups project to different sub-regions of V2 and from there to different sets of extrastriate areas: The ventral (temporal) pathway that includes area V4 and the inferotemporal cortex (IT); and the dorsal (parietal) pathway that includes the middle temporal (MT) and parietal areas. The dorsal pathway (*where* pathway) processes information about spatial location and motion, and the ventral pathway (*what* pathway) is specific for color and form processing (Ungerleider and Mishkin, 1982). Thus, the distinction between *what* and *where* in the brain roughly starts with information of M and P cells in the retina. Then, information about *what* takes the ventral pathway, while information for *where* is processed in the dorsal pathway. Note that the idea of two completely separate and independent pathways is an oversimplification, albeit generally correct, since there are many anatomical connections that create 'cross-talk' between these pathways in the cortex.

Feature maps are not only present in V1, but also in areas V4 and MT. Information represented by feature detectors increases in complexity in higher-level visual areas, with neurons representing more complex information but with less spatial selectivity than neurons in V1. For example, neurons in V4 and IT seem to be selective for complex combinations of color and orientation, and for complex combination of shape features. Moreover, some neurons in IT seem to even code for specific faces. These higher ventral visual areas are, at the same time, less spatially selective: Their receptive fields cover expansive positions of the visual field and they are therefore less sensitive to the position of the stimuli, or, in other words, they seem to be location invariant. For example, a V4 neuron that fires strongly when a red vertical bar is located on the center of its receptive field would fire as strongly if the same object is on the right or on the left part of its receptive field. By contrast, neurons in higher dorsal areas are selective for motion and spatial location. Also in this case, the information processed is more complex than the one processed in V1: Some neurons within MT respond selectively to the direction of entire objects' motion. Neurons in the parietal cortex are selective for object's location in head and body centered, rather than retinal, coordinates.

Thus, the visual system is both a hierarchical system, with the complexity of the processed information increasing higher-up in the system; and a parallel system, with information being processed in parallel by separate channels and being represented by multiple different feature maps. An area that fully combines all the details of such distributed information does not seem to exist (but see Rao *et al.*, 1997). Creating a coherent representation of the visual world, then, seems to require an additional active mechanism that coordinates the activity in such feature maps.

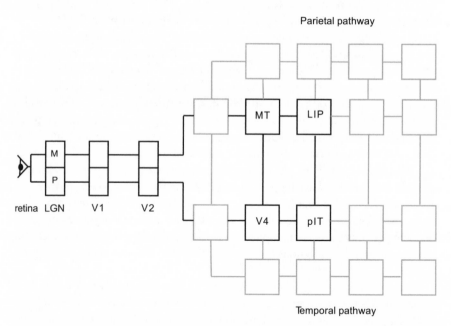

Fig. 3.2: The structure of the visual system. Two distinct pathways in the LGN convey information from the retina to the primary visual cortex (V1): The M pathway analyzes motion, and the P pathway analyzes color and form. This functional segregation is roughly maintained in higher-level areas of the cortical visual system, where 'extra-striate' cortical areas are organized into two parallel pathways: The temporal pathway leading over area V4 to the inferior temporal (IT) cortex and the parietal pathway leading over area MT to the posterior parietal cortex (including area LIP). Cortical areas of major interest are represented by black boxes; their connections are represented by black lines. Gray boxes represent further unspecified areas. Note that connections between the parietal and temporal pathways exist at several levels.

3.2 The Binding Problem in Vision

Before considering which kind of mechanism actively binds features in order to create objects' representations, it is useful to distinguish among different types of binding, since their solution might be accomplished by different kinds of mechanisms:

- Binding of elementary features across space: This is the binding of elements belonging to the same object across different positions.
- Binding across feature dimensions: This is the binding of independently coded features (e.g., color, orientation, and motion) belonging to the same object at a specific location.
- Binding of *what* and *where*: This is a higher-level binding that links the representation of object's identity to the representation of its location in space.

The binding of elementary features across space has been extensively studied in the context of perceptual grouping. It seems to depend on 'perceptual rules' that hinge on regularities of the visual world. For example, we perceive adjacent edges with similar orientation as part of the same object. In fact, in the visual world such a pattern of edges, normally, defines an object's border. Gestalt psychologists were the first to define principles underlying perceptual grouping (e.g., Kanisza, 1979). Recent neurophysiological works have provided evidence for the neural mechanism underlying some of these principles (Gray, 1999; Gilbert and Sigman, 2007). For example, it has been found that the responses of V1 neurons to stimuli in their receptive fields are modulated by the context: A neuron responds strongly to an oriented bar if this bar is embedded in a contour of collinear bars located outside of its receptive field.

Perceptual grouping describes how the visual system integrates features across space by means of rules that have been acquired through experience. But surely, our visual system can also represent objects defined by any combination of features, even if this combination has never been seen before. It is unlikely that such a binding of features depends on stored perceptual rules, making mechanisms underlying perceptual grouping not apt to explain this type of binding. My interest is in how the visual system accomplishes this type of binding that is required for binding of features at a specific location and for binding of *what* and *where*. Particularly, I am going to focus on binding across feature dimensions (*feature conjunction*) because it has been studied empirically in greater detail. I will first consider the empirical evidence for and against the existence of a 'binding problem' and for its solution through an active mechanism.

Early psychophysical evidence for the existence of a feature conjunction problem in vision came from studies of visual search (Treisman and Gelade, 1980). It was noticed that it takes much longer to find a target stimulus among distractors if it only differs from distractors in terms of a conjunction of features, than if it

differs in terms of a single unique feature. For example, subjects quickly detect a
red-vertical bar among green bars but it takes longer to find this red-vertical bar
if it is embedded in red-horizontal and green-vertical bars (fig. 3.3). Salient features tend to 'pop out' from the array, while feature conjunction seems to require
scrutiny in order to be found. Treisman and Gelade interpreted the differences
in search times as reflecting two different mechanisms: A pre-attentive and fast
mechanism detecting elementary features, and a slow – serial – search mechanism
for conjoining features.[1]

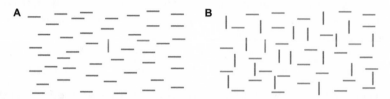

Fig. 3.3: Visual search. (A) In feature search, the red bar 'pops-out' when embedded in green and
horizontal bars. (B) By contrast, in a conjunction search, the same red bar is much harder to detect,
since it can only be distinguished from the distractors by a conjunction of color and orientation.

Studies of 'illusory conjunctions' provided further psychophysical evidence for
the existence of a feature conjunction problem (Treisman and Gelade, 1980;
Treisman and Schmidt, 1982). Illusory conjunctions are perceptual illusions, in
which features belonging to different briefly presented objects are erroneously
combined. For example, by briefly presenting two bars, a subject in most cases will
report a wrong combination of the features characterizing the bars. That is to say,
a subject can detect which features are in the scene but she fails to correctly report
how the features are conjoint, so that the report can be that there are, for example,
a green-vertical bar and a red-horizontal bar, while, instead, a red-vertical bar and
a green-horizontal bar were briefly presented. Treisman and Gelade hypothesized
that such illusory conjunctions only occur if the visual system processes features
separately, and if a slow attentional mechanism is required to conjoin features. It
has later been objected that illusory conjunctions might occur because subjects do
not have enough time for building up a persistent representation of the stimulus,
which allows for perceptual report. Thus, illusory conjunctions might reflect a
memory failure rather than a true perceptual mis-binding (Wolfe and Cave, 1999).

Stronger evidence for this type of mis-binding comes from studies of a patient
suffering from Balint's syndrome (Friedman-Hill et al., 1995).[2] This patient per-

---

[1] Some authors (e.g., Wolfe, 1994) argue that the difference in visual search performance between
single unique feature and conjunction search might be explained by a saliency mechanism, rather
than a binding mechanism.

[2] Balint's syndrome results from bilateral damage of the parietal cortex and manifests itself in terms of
almost complete loss of spatial awareness: A patient with Balint's syndrome perceives an object at

ceived illusory conjunctions when presented with displayed objects, even when these were displayed for long durations (up to ten seconds). This study clears doubts related to short time presentation and argues for a binding problem solved by attention.

As opposed to Treisman and Gelade's findings, evidence for an automatic binding at the early stages of the visual process has been provided. Using an adaptation paradigm, Blaser and colleagues (2005) found that conjunctions of color and motion elicited a specific aftereffect (a 'color-contingent motion after-effect'). Interestingly, they found that this aftereffect occurred at an early level of motion processing (perhaps in V1), and was unaffected by feedback from higher-order direction-sensitive areas, such as MT and downstream areas. Their study suggests that simple features, such as color and motion, are processed conjointly rather than independently at early stages of the visual system, and, thus, that there might, in fact, be no binding problem for this kind of feature conjunction at all.

However, Wu and colleagues (2004) using similar stimuli found evidence for conjunctions of color and motion. Specifically, two superimposed surfaces made of colored moving dots are presented, in which, for example, upward motion is combined with red and downward motion with green. The stimulus is such that if dots of one color in the center of the screen move upwards then dots of that color in periphery move downwards, and vice versa. Subjects tend to see the same conjunction of features in the periphery as in the center; namely, they perceive red and green dots as moving upward and downward, respectively, even though the physical motion is quite the opposite. This study suggests that features, such as color and motion, are processed independently and their conjunction require an attentive mechanism.

3.3 Potential Binding Mechanisms

The studies discussed above seem to suggest that the binding problem is in fact a real problem for the visual brain, and not only a scientific construct. This substantiates the conclusions from the study of the functional architecture of the visual system, namely, that an active mechanism is normally at play that coordinates the representations carried by the feature maps. What might this mechanism be?

Different models have been proposed. They can be divided into two main groups: (*i*) Static binding models; and (*ii*) dynamic binding models. Dynamic binding models can be further divided according to whether they describe the

---

a time without being able to locate it in space. For example, while looking at an object moving, he cannot report the direction of motion.

binding mechanism at a functional level, such as Treisman and Gelade's 'Feature Integration Theory' (1980); or they describe this mechanism at a neural level, such as Singer and Gray's 'binding by synchrony hypothesis' (1995). These dynamic binding models are not mutually exclusive: A general solution of the binding problem might emerge from a synthesis of functional and neural models (see Section 3.3.3).

3.3.1 *Static binding models: the hypothesis of 'binding by convergence'*

Static models of shape binding postulate that binding is simply achieved by the successive construction of progressively complex representations of visual stimuli along the hierarchy of the ventral visual pathway (Hubel and Wiesel, 1968; Barlow, 1972; Riesenhuber and Poggio, 1999). Specifically, simple feature selective detectors in V1, such as orientation detectors, might converge in a specific way onto neurons in higher ventral areas, which, then, respond selectively to more complex conjunctions of shape features. Ultimately, the information converges onto, so-called, 'grandmother cells' responding to specific conjunctions of features that uniquely identify a particular object. An often-cited evidence for the existence of such 'grandmother cells' is the existence in IT of neurons specifically coding for particular faces.

However, binding by convergence does not seem to provide a general solution for all the aspects of the visual binding problem described above. There do not seem to be enough neurons available in the brain to uniquely encode all the different objects we are able to see: Think about the number of different viewpoints from which we can consider a single object, and, then, consider that a similar number applies for almost all the objects we see. All different views of an object would need to be somehow explicitly encoded by distinct neurons in the static binding scheme, and, ultimately, shape reconstruction – the representation of object's identity (*what*) – has to be combined with the representation of their location (*where*). The combination of *what* and *where* requires an even more complex structure, for which no basis seems to exist in the primate brain.

Thus, it appears that a more flexible, and truly active, mechanism is required to provide a general solution for all facets of the binding problem.

3.3.2 *Dynamic binding models*

Several models of object representation assume that the representation of an object is not encoded by few single neurons but is distributed across a large group of neurons located in distinct areas. The idea of distributed representations by neuronal groups has been originally proposed by Hebb (1949): If the activity of a neuron correlates regularly with the activity of other neurons, the connections between these neurons will be strengthened. Thus, learning creates groups of neurons (*cell assemblies*). One advantage of such a distributed coding scheme is its efficiency in terms of the number of neurons required: Each cell can, at different times, take part in the representation of different objects, depending on the assembly which it is currently part of. Hebb's theory is now a common paradigm in neurophysiological and computational studies of the visual system.

Taking the distributed nature of neural representations as a starting point, how, then, can these distributed neural representations be linked into a coherent object representation? I will now consider two models of such an active binding process: Feature Integration Theory and binding by synchrony.

3.3.2.1 Feature Integration Theory (FIT)

Feature integration theory was developed based on findings from studies of visual search and illusory conjunction paradigms that I discussed above.[3] According to FIT, the binding of separated coded features depends on directing attention to a given object in space. The model distinguishes between two stages: A parallel (pre-attentive) stage at which single unique features are rapidly detected, and a serial (attentive) stage at which features are combined in order to create object representations (fig. 3.4).

Local elementary features are separately represented in multiple topographic features maps. Single unique features in the visual field can be rapidly detected through large signals in one of these maps. Therefore, in single feature search the target is immediately detected and in feature conjunction search, the scene is scrutinized serially before a target can be detected. In order to bind features together for identifying an object, it is necessary to select information in feature maps through an active attentional mechanism. Specifically, when the focus of attention selects a particular location of the image, only the features occurring at this location gain access to a higher stage of object recognition. When confronted with a cluttered visual scene, visual attention serially scans through a 'master-map' of locations (or saliency map), and the features at the currently selected location are conjoined in order to form a full representation of the attended object.

In FIT, feature binding is an intermediate process of visual object perception that is succeeded by object recognition, that is, a comparison of the bound representation with memorized objects.

---

[3] The original Feature Integration Theory has been considerably revised over the years to account for new findings that challenged parts of the theory (Treisman, 1993). However, the basic attentional mechanism postulated by FIT remains the same: Features maps are selected through spatial attention by means of connections among a location (saliency) map in the dorsal pathway and the feature maps themselves.

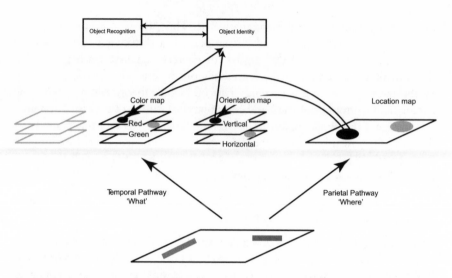

Fig. 3.4: Feature integration theory (FIT). Information about the visual scene is processed in parallel by the temporal ('what') and parietal ('where') pathways. In the 'what' pathway feature information is represented in topographic maps in a pre-attentive stage. An attentional mechanism is necessary to bind the features when two or more objects are present in the scene: Spatial attention selects a particular location in a location map of the 'where' pathway and binds (through the connections with the corresponding locations in the feature maps) the features of the object at that location. These features are, therefore bound into a coherent object representation, which can then be recognized through comparison with stored representations. In this figure, attention selects the area defined by the black circle (corresponding to the position of the red-vertical bar) and a signal is sent to the feature maps for red and vertical. Note that the spatial arrangement of the activations for red and vertical in the color and orientation maps corresponds to the selected location in the location map. During visual conjunction search, attention scans through the location map and selects location by location in order to find the target object (adapted from Treisman, 1993). Note that in this figure the location map is located in the dorsal pathway, as described in Treisman (1993). However, which area contributes to the representation of location (or saliency at that location) is still an open question (e.g., Koch & Ullman (1985); Robinson & Petersen, 1992; Gottlieb, 2007).

3.3.2.2 Binding by synchrony

The binding by synchrony hypothesis was originally developed to account for perceptual grouping (Von der Malsburg, 1981) but was later also proposed as a possible mechanism for feature conjunction (Crick and Koch, 1990; Singer and Gray, 1995). The hypothesis is that neurons encoding features belonging to the same object synchronize their responses, and desynchronize their responses from neurons encoding features of different objects. Synchrony of neuronal responses thus 'tags' neuronal activities belonging to the same object representation by a temporal code (fig. 3.5).

Several physiological studies have been conducted to investigate the role of synchrony of neuronal activity in perceptual grouping and feature binding, with highly discrepant outcomes (Gray *et al.*, 1989; Engel *et al.*, 1991; Lamme and Spekreijse, 1998; Thiele and Stoner, 2003; Palanca and De Angelis, 2005). Among them, one of the most influential studies in support of this hypothesis was an experiment by Gray and colleagues (1989). This group of researchers recorded the activity of two neurons, sensitive to the same orientation, with non-overlapping receptive field, in the primary visual cortex of anesthetized cats. The cats were presented with (*i*) two bars with identical orientations moving either in opposite directions, or in the same direction, and with (*ii*) a long bar moving across the fields of the recorded cells. According to the binding by synchrony hypothesis, neurons should synchronize their activity if the two stimuli passing through the receptive fields belong to the same object. Gray and colleagues found the highest synchronization of neuronal activity for the single long bar, an intermediate level of synchronization when two bars moved in the same direction, and no synchronization when two bars moved in opposite directions. These results are consistent with the hypothesis that neuronal synchrony is modulated with the perceptual grouping of local features. Additionally, the same group observed that the activity of neurons that synchronize tends to become oscillatory, and that these neuronal oscillations are often expressed in the 'gamma'-frequency range (40–100 Hz; Gray and Singer, 1989; Engel and Singer, 2001).

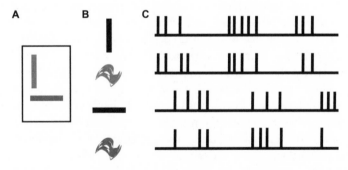

Fig. 3.5: The 'binding by synchrony' model. The visual scene (A) is decomposed into primitive features represented by distinct neuronal groups (B). Feature binding depends on the synchronous activity of neurons representing features that belong to the same object: (C) Neurons encoding the red and vertical bar synchronize their activity and de-synchronize their activity from neurons representing the green and horizontal bar.

The hypothesis has subsequently been challenged by theoretical arguments (Shadlen and Movshon, 1999) and empirical findings (Lamme and Spekreijse, 1998; Thiele and Stoner, 2003; Palanca and De Angelis, 2005). Specifically, Lamme and Spekreijse (1998) found no systematic relationship between synchrony of cells in V1 and figure-ground segregation and perceptual grouping. Instead, they reported a strong correlation between the firing rates of V1 neurons and these perceptual processes. Thiele and Stoner (2003) and Palanca and De Angelis (2005) found no evidence for synchrony underlying binding of visual motion signals.

3.3.3 *How binding by attention and binding by synchrony can be reconciled*

The dynamic models so far described consider two distinct levels of description: FIT provides a functional explanation of feature binding, in which binding operations are defined according to their functional roles. The binding by synchrony hypothesis provides an explanation of feature binding at a neural level. Therefore these accounts are not mutually exclusive (Crick and Koch, 1990; Treisman, 1996). In fact, synchronization of neuronal activity might be the neuronal mechanism by which attention selects sensory signals for further processing (Salinas and Sejnowski, 2001).

Reynolds and Desimone (1999) argue that neurophysiological evidence supports the role of attention in feature binding. As we have seen, neurons in higher-level ventral visual areas, like V4 and IT, have large receptive fields that typically contain multiple objects when our visual system is presented with a cluttered visual scene. A neuron in one of these areas can respond to multiple features, firing strongly whenever its preferred features are within its receptive field. However, if the neuron's receptive field contains more than one object at a time, it is hard to disentangle to which of these objects the neuron responds. Suppose, for example, that a neuron responds to both red and vertical: When these features (carried either by a unique object or carried by two distinct objects) are within its receptive field, the neuron fires strongly. Thus, if a red and vertical bar is signaled, the activity of the neuron increases but the neuron will also fire (even if less strongly) when a green and vertical bar is in its receptive field, since vertical is one of its preferred features. Moreover, if two stimuli, like a red-horizontal bar and a green-vertical bar, are within the neuron's receptive field, the neuron will fire strongly since both its preferred features are signaled, making hard to disentangle which features belong to the two stimuli (fig. 3.6a/b). Which of the two stimuli does the neuron encode? The response of these higher-order neurons to multiple objects seems to be ambiguous. How, then, can subsequent stages of the visual pathway decode this signal? Recordings of neurons in area V4 and IT of awake behaving monkeys suggest that attention plays a role in the *disambiguation* of neuronal responses (Moran and Desimone, 1984; Reynolds and Desimone, 1999). When presented with two objects in the receptive field, the response of V4 and IT neurons seem to only reflect the features of the object the monkey is currently attending to: If the attended stimulus carries neuron's preferred features, the neuron increases its activity. If the attended stimulus carries non-preferred features, the neuron's activity decreases even though the stimulus defined by its preferred features is still in its receptive field. For example, when both a red vertical bar and a green horizontal bar are within a neuron's receptive field, the activity of the neuron depends on which of the two stimuli is attended: If attention is directed towards the red-vertical bar, the neuron respond strongly, ignoring completely the presence of the green-horizontal bar in its receptive field; vice versa, when the focus of attention is the green-horizontal bar, the part of neurons' receptive field in which the red-vertical bar is located is ignored (fig. 3.6c/d).

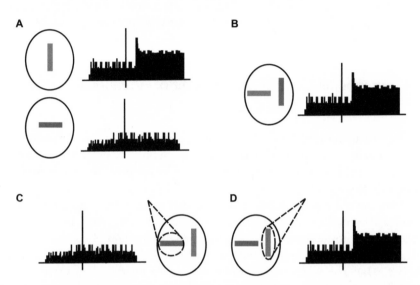

Fig. 3.6: A potential role of the neural mechanism of attention in the *disambiguation* of neuronal responses. (A) A neuron in a higher-ventral area (V4 or IT) responds strongly to its preferred features – red and vertical – and does not response to non-preferred features – green and horizontal. (B) The activity of the neuron is strong when two stimuli carrying the preferred features are within its receptive field, making impossible to discern which features belong to which of the two objects. (C, D) Spatial attention enhances the effective spatial resolution of the neuron, thereby disambiguating its signal: (C) When the focus of attention is on the non-preferred stimulus, the neuron decreases its activity, as if only the green and vertical bar were in its receptive field; (D) when attention is focused on the preferred stimulus, the neuron fires strongly as if only the red and vertical bar were present in its receptive field.

Thus, the neuron effectively behaves as if only the attended object is present in the visual field. These results suggest that attention mediates a 'shrinkage' of neurons' large receptive fields around the attended object and thereby disambiguates the information carried by those neurons' responses. In other words, "attention solves the binding problem by increasing the effective spatial resolution of the visual system so that even neurons with multiple stimuli inside their receptive fields process information only about stimuli at the attended location (Reynolds and Desimone, 1999, p. 20)." How is this 'shrinkage' of receptive fields achieved?

Fries and colleagues (2001) hypothesized that the synchrony of neuronal responses in the visual cortex might gate selected visual inputs to further stages. To test this hypothesis, Fries and colleagues recorded neurons in area V4 of a macaque monkey, while the monkey was attending for one of two stimuli in the visual field. They found that the synchrony of neuronal activity was enhanced with spatial attention. This selective modulation of neuronal synchronization by spatial attention might be instrumental in the selection of currently relevant stimuli for further processing, leading the functional shrinking of receptive fields at the subsequent stage. Siegel and colleagues made a similar finding in the human brain (Siegel *et al.*, 2008): They report that spatial attention modulates neuronal synchrony along the dorsal visual pathway.

3.4 Attentional Control and the Unit of Attentional Selection

So far I have considered spatial attention as a potential mechanism underlying feature binding. Let us now consider how attention is controlled and whether the unit of attentional selection is solely location in space or a more complex representation.

How does the brain decide which location to attend to? According to an influential hypothesis, a topographically organized 'saliency map' (similar to the location map postulated in FIT; fig. 3.4) represents location of conspicuous and behaviorally relevant stimuli in the visual field (Koch and Ullman, 1985; Itti and Koch, 2001). This saliency map, which might be located in the parietal cortex, combines inputs from multiple feature maps: "Saliency at a given location is determined primarily by how different this location is from its surround in color, orientation, motion, depth, etc. (Koch and Ullman, 1985, p. 221)" but it can also be determined by our current goals like, for example, whether we are searching for a green or a red object (Wolfe, 1994). A 'winner take-all' mechanism, then, determines the most salient location in this map. This leads to a feedback signal to the corresponding locations within feature maps, namely, to the expression of attention in the visual cortex. This is achieved through the feedback connections from parietal and frontal areas to visual cortex. These feedback inputs, then, enhance the activity of neurons corresponding to the feature maps in such a way that their activities synchronize (Crick and Koch, 1990).

The psychophysical and neurophysiological evidence discussed above suggests that spatial attention plays a predominant role in feature binding. Nevertheless, recent studies suggest that attentional effects cannot be attributed to spatial selection alone. Instead, they seem to reflect the selection of already integrated objects (Pylyshyn and Storm, 1988; Blaser *et al.*, 2000). These results challenge feature integration theory and other attention-based binding models because they seem to suggest that some form of binding exists even prior to attention.

An experiment by Pylsyhyn and Storm (1988) with Multiple Object Tracking (MOT) provided evidence for object-based attention. In this experiment, eight identical and randomly moving dots are shown. Subjects' task was to keep track of a subset of target-defined dots, which were indicated by temporarily flickering the dots or temporarily changing their color, and to indicate, at the end of the experiment, which were the original targets. Results showed that subjects could track up to five independently moving targets. The authors argued that spatial attention cannot be the mechanism behind tracking, since it is a serial mechanism that selects one location at a time, and, in the experiment, dots randomly moved preventing the switching of attention to different locations. Thus, the accuracy of a subject's tracking cannot be explained by a purely spatial attentional mechanism. Instead, Pylyshyn (1989, 2001) argues for an object-based primitive mechanism in early vision that selects, tracks and maintains the identity of individual objects: a FINST (Finger of Instantiation), or visual index. Visual indexes are conceived as pointers that point from an encoded representation of an object to an actual object.[4] Such a pointer would allow updating the previously encoded representation of the object with new perceived properties. Visual indexes are assigned depending on the saliency of the visual objects in the distal scene through a mechanism that is similar to the saliency map mechanism described above (Pylyshyn and Eagleson, 1994).

The hypothesis of FINST is thought to provide an alternative mechanism for individuating visual features and for indexing (or binding) these features to a particular location within the visual field without assuming an explicit encoding of feature types or encoding of locations in a coordinate system. Thus, visual indexes do not carry information about which object they are pointing to and where this object is located: Their role is to allow higher cognitive processes to refer to some specific indexed features in order to evaluate the spatial relations among them (Pylyshyn, 1989). However, many of the assumptions involved in the FINST idea are not conclusive and need further empirical exploration (see, for example, Scholl, 2009).

3.5 Models of Object Recognition

So far I have dealt with approaches studying the binding problem in simple visual scenes. However, feature binding is only a stage of a more complex process that leads to object recognition. Even if my primary interest is not in this particular stage of the visual processing, the description of models of visual object recognition helps in clarifying how earlier visual processes, like binding, are related to the perception of the visual world.

---

[4] Visual indexes are considered to act as demonstratives (*this, that*), which allow referring to a particular individual in a cluttered scene without the need to encode all the properties of the scene.

Different models of visual object recognition have been postulated (Marr, 1982; Biederman, 1987; Treisman, 1993). They all account for how the visual system extracts and combines features at different stages but they diverge in defining the role of each stage.

According to FIT, object perception depends on the interaction between feature maps, a 'master-map' of location, and object files (Treisman, 1993, fig.3.4). The interaction between spatial attention and feature maps explains how feature binding might be accomplished: There is a first, pre-attentive, stage in which features are represented separately in feature maps. Attention-based binding of information from the feature maps results in the representation of the attended object. This is followed by another attentional stage, which is based on object selection. Treisman posits a high-level attentional process that selects the perceptual object and stores object-related information in a representation – an object file – that includes all the properties of the object. The object file represents the current state of an object and updates it when the object moves or changes. This stage is necessary to account for the view invariance of object recognition.

The hypothesis of object files is also part of Pylyshyn's FINST theory. However, there is a main difference between FIT and FINST: FIT postulates a binding process that depends on spatial attention, whereas FINST allows only for object-based selection. In FIT, once an object has been selected in an object file, the location of this object can be maintained by links between the object file and the master-map of location; whereas in FINST, the object file is constantly updated by successive scans of the tracked object in the visual scene.

FIT is based on a hierarchical structure that goes from an early stage of feature extraction to object recognition. This structure is common to other models of object recognition. For example, Marr's computational theory (Marr, 1982) attempts to explain how the three-dimensional image is reconstructed from information coming from the retina. According to Marr's theory, object recognition has several computational stages, each of which carries a specific task in the reconstruction of a stable and view-independent object. The process starts with the extraction of primitive features according to differences in the intensity of the image. The set of primary features is composed by edges, blobs, and lines. Features that are similar in size and orientation are grouped, according to Gestalt rules of perceptual organization and physical regularities, in subsequent stages until they are transformed into a three-dimensional representation of the object. The focus of Marr's computational approach is to analyze how the visual system construct a stable and view-invariant representation of the visual object. As we have seen, models of static binding specifically deal with these questions. Several attempts to implement Marr's theory with static binding model have been put forward (see, for example, Riesenhuber and Poggio, 1999).

Structural models of object recognition also address how view-invariant representations are build up in the visual system. Those models are influenced by

Biederman's recognition by component (RBC; Biederman, 1987). RBC is based on the idea that object recognition starts with features extraction that lead to the definition of a primitive set of three-dimensional visual representations – *Geons* (Geometric Ions). If the visual system can retrieve enough information to identify Geons that constitute an objects then it is possible to identify that object. Thus, combinations of Geons are necessary to represent the object perceived. This representation is, then, matched with representations stored in memory for recognition. As opposed to approaches based on static binding, RBC only necessitates a limited number of Geons to reconstruct visual objects. Implementation of RBC can be made either by static binding models (Biederman, 1987) or by architecture that implements a combined static-dynamic approach (Hummel, 2001). Nevertheless, RCB might fail to account for some visual properties such as perceiving subtle differences among similar objects. In fact, Geons might not be sufficiently fine-grained to capture the richness of visual representations. To take an example: Birds' beaks are all represented by the same Geon but every beak differs for dimension, taper, etc. A single Geon might fail to capture these diversities. At the same time, selection for detailed features seems to be a basic property of neurons.

3.6 Conclusion

The analysis of the functional architecture of the visual system and the binding problem in vision helps sharpening the notion of visual primitive representations and of the structure of the processes underlying the integration of these representations. Psychophysical and physiological evidence argues for a set of primitive visual representations that stand for features of objects in the external world.

The analysis of binding mechanisms shows that the binding process involves more than a simple association of features. In the case of attention, features are conjoined by means of their location; whereas for binding by synchrony, a temporal tag identifies features belonging to the same object. It has been argued that feature binding through attention can be described as 'Here (x, y)' and 'There (h, z)' (Clark, 2000) and binding of synchrony as 'This (x,y)' and 'That (h, z)' (Werning, 2005). I am going to evaluate both accounts in the next chapter. I will, then, provide a description of the binding process based on the evidence provided in this chapter and on the initial account of visual object perception as a process on non-conceptual representations.

4
Systematicity of Visual Binding

Before explaining in detail why visual feature binding is systematic, it is useful to briefly recapitulate the main ideas discussed so far:

1) Vision is a system of non-conceptual mental representations.

2) Evidence from neuroscience suggests that vision is a structured process, mostly because of the dynamic nature of the binding processes underlying object representation.

According to a common assumption in philosophy, the structure of sensory systems, and specifically vision, fundamentally differs from the structure of higher cognition (Evans, 1982). Because of this structural differences vision does not satisfy the requirements of the Generality Constraint (Heck, 2007). To reiterate, the Generality Constraint states that an individual that is able to be in the representational state that a is F and b is G is also able to be in the structurally related representational state that a is G and b is F.[1] Vision lacks the causal combinatorial structure typical of higher cognition that underlies the systematicity of a system behavior. In contrast with the philosophically accepted model of cognition and based on empirical evidence from neuroscientific studies of the binding problem, I am going to argue that visual feature binding shows a systematic behavior, too.

For a system to be systematic, primitive representations need to be causally related, so that the representation resulting from their combination contains these primitive representations as constituents, and so as parts. In addition, if the resulting representation has other representations as constituents, then it is a complex representation. Similarly, early structural models of visual object recognition postulate a set of primitive constituents, on which the further computations underlying the representation of three-dimensional objects are performed (Marr and Nishihara, 1978). A typical structural theory, such as Biederman's Recognition by Components (1987), describes object recognition as resulting from the combination of simple geometrical components according to specific spatial relations. For example, the representation of a cup depends on the combination of two different spatially arranged components: the representation of the handle and the representation of the body of the cup. The need to posit a set of primitive visual constituents is a consequence of the limited computational resources of brain pro-

---

[1] Evans originally formulated the Generality Constraint to account for the structure of thought, rather than to account for the general structure of mental representations. Because of the relation between the Generality Constraint and systematicity, one can think of the Generality Constraint as a general property of symbolic representational states.

cesses (von der Malsburg, 1981). For example, the representation of every possible configuration of objects in a visual scene by corresponding neurons would require a number of neurons that exceeds their actual number in the visual cortex. The flexible recombination of a limited set of constituents avoids this problem. I will discuss below why combinatorial processes on structured primitive constituents are systematic (and compositional, in the next chapter).

The effectiveness of structural models to account for cognitive processes and visual object recognition has been criticized on empirical, computational, and theoretical grounds (Edelman, 1997; Palmeri and Gauthier, 2004). For example, the extraction of volumetric primitives – i. e., the extraction of geons that are created by combining simple features like edges and vertices – posits a challenging problem to computational vision scientists. Early structural models bypass the problem of feature extraction, failing to explain how the visual system reliably extracts edges and vertices to represent geons. Moreover, these models ignore metric information about size and shape, making fine discrimination among objects difficult. The lack of a proper definition of a set of primitive constituents weakens the role of structural models of object recognition in explaining the systematic behavior of the visual system.

In this chapter, I am going to propose an alternative account of the systematicity of visual object perception by considering visual feature binding operations (binding by attention and synchrony) required for successful object recognition.[2] My aim is to show that visual feature binding is a combinatorial spatial process that displays systematicity. It will turn out, thus, that visual feature binding implements a structure of constituents, which fulfills the requirements of the Generality Constraint, while lacking the descriptive structure of higher cognitive processes.

I begin with some remarks on the primitive constituents of vision and their content.

4.1 Visual Primitive Constituents

The primitive constituents of the object representation that results from visual binding operations, are, the so-called, *features* represented by the activity of topographic *feature maps* in early visual cortex. The operational definition of a basic feature was first provided in perceptual psychology based on studies of visual search and texture segmentation (Wolfe, 1998). First, a basic feature allows for efficient visual search when embedded in a cluttered scene of unlike distracters.

---

[2] Object recognition is a dynamic process. However, the process itself is better understood when considered within a hierarchical structure so that it is easier to distinguish earlier processes from the later ones. Nevertheless, early processes might have an influence, or an active role, to represent information in visual scene perception.

The efficiency of visual search is indicated by the so-called 'pop-out' of the target that reflects an underlying parallel process, which operates automatically and throughout the visual field. In contrast, targets distinguished from distracters by a combination of basic features require a longer time to be found; time that increases with the number of distracters presented in the scene. Second, a basic feature supports effortless texture segregation. For example, a region of vertical lines in a field of horizontal lines will be immediately segregated from the background and perceived as a figure. Color, orientation, and motion clearly justify the criteria of efficient search and effortless segmentation, and are, thus, accepted as primitive features.[3] Thus, basic visual features are the primitive constituents of visual feature binding.[4] The operational definition of basic feature is consolidated by neurophysiological findings of the organization of the visual system. Neurophysiological results suggest that several retinotopically organized visual areas are made of groups of local feature detectors. In each feature map, the feature detectors represent the occurrence of a specific feature in their preferred location of the visual field. Thus, these detectors represent the value of a specific feature at a specific location.

The reported psychophysical and physiological studies point to features represented by feature maps as the primitive visual constituents of feature binding. Feature maps topographically represent color, motion, and orientation, and, perhaps, other features. However, because of their topographic organization, feature maps represent not only the value of features but also their location. For example, whenever a subject perceives a green-horizontal bar in the right upper corner of the visual field, detectors in the corresponding retinotopic position of the feature maps 'green' and 'vertical' are active. Feature maps, then, represent two kinds of information: *(i)* the type of feature, and *(ii)* its location in the visual field.

Recent works in philosophy account for the representational content of perceptual experience in terms of ways of filling out the space around a perceiver. This is the case, for example, of Peacocke's *scenario content* (1992b). Scenario contents are basic forms of representational content individuated by the correspondence between specific characteristics of the external world in a determinate location and the content of the scenario:

> The idea is that the content involves a spatial *type*, the type being that under which fall precisely those ways of filling the space around the subject which are consistent with the correctness of the content. On this model, correctness of content is then a matter of

---

[3] Wolfe (1998) provides a more comprehensive list of candidates for primitive features, which are still debated, including: Curvature, Vernier offset, size, spatial frequency, scale, and shape. Among these features, shape is the most problematic, mostly because of the lack of a widely agreed understanding of what corresponds to the *shape space* (Wolfe, 1998, p. 33).

[4] From now on, I will interchangeably use the terms 'visual features' and 'visual constituents' to identify the primitive constituents of the binding process.

instantiation: the instantiation by the real world around the perceiver of the spatial type which gives the representational content in question. (Peacocke, 1992b, p. 105; *italics CP*).

Similarly, Clark (2000) argues that sensory systems, *qua* representational systems, employ a basic form of mental representations that indicate the appearance of a feature at a certain region. In the case of vision, the placing of a feature secures the perceived identity of an object. That is to say, we perceive features occurring at the same place as being related to the same object. A consequence of this approach is to consider sensory experience as being *about* location:

> [...] If one is asked 'What are sensory states *about*? What is the subject-matter of sensory representation?' the answer I suggest is, invariably, 'Space-time regions of finite but definite extent, in or around the body of the sentient organism'. [...] The sensation is a sensation *of* that region; the sensation is what the representation σ is *about*. (Clark, 2000, p. 109; *italics AC*).

I am unease with equating the importance of location to integrate features with the claim that the content of sensory representation is about location. Nevertheless, the representation of location in early visual areas seems to be critical for the resulting representation of an object (Wandell *et al.*, 2007).[5] My point is that feature maps represent both object features and their location: *How* exactly do feature maps represent location? Is location a primitive feature?

According to the definition of feature given above, location is not a feature: There is neither a visual search for a location, nor can location segregate from a background. However, information about location is clearly represented in the brain: Visual early cortical areas represent both information of feature values and feature locations. The ventral pathway is thought to carry information about the identity of objects, as opposed to the dorsal pathway, which carries information about motion and location. But feature maps in the early stages of the ventral pathway (V1 to V4) represent the location of features in addition to the information of the values of features. The accuracy of information about *where* features are located is reduced and eventually lost in higher hierarchical stages of the ventral visual pathway. Thus, the ending product of the ventral system is an object representation detached from its spatial position. Nevertheless, in visual scenes, objects are always perceived at their location. In fact, we are normally able to report where an object is. This ability is often expressed by the use of referring expression, such as 'There it is', and so on. To this extent, information about location needs somehow to be maintained. How this is accomplished becomes clear as soon as we go through the details of the structure of visual binding operations.

---

[5] In contrast to this view, one can say that the visual system does not need to represent location information to represent an object. As an example, see the description of object-based attention in chapter three, and Section 4.4 in this chapter.

4.2 Why Vision is Apparently not Systematic

For a system to be systematic, it is necessary that a particular relation hold among a complex representation and its constituents: The relation of constituency. Constituency is a mereological relation, according to which primitive representations have a causal role in the construction of the complex representation. The causal role is specified by the constituents being tokened whenever the complex representation is tokened. Failure in explicitly representing one of the constituents results in failure of representing a complex representation in which this constituent might be involved. For example, a subject with a *punctate mind* (Fodor and Pylyshyn, 1988) can represent the state of affairs *a is F* and *b is G* but fail to represent the structurally related state of affairs *a is G* and *b is F*. This subject cannot grasp the mental representations F and G, thus, she is unable to have systematic mental representations (Fodor, 1996).

Two main arguments support the hypothesis that vision fails to have a structure of constituents and, thus, lacks systematicity. The first argument derives from considering the structures of vision and cognition. Serial cognitive processes have a combinatorial structure of constituents: Their structure is such that the constituents are not only associated with the final representation but also are actual parts of it. Instead, distributed processes are often characterized as associative (Clark, Andy, 1993); namely, they lack a systematic behavior. By extension, vision, as a parallel distributed and hierarchically organized system, fails to implement a structure of constituents and the resulting systematicity.

The second argument is based on Evans' characterization of the structure of thought. Thoughts are structured in a way that satisfies the Generality Constraint. Thus, whenever a subject grasps a representation with a specific content, this representation can be recombined in different structural relations. It is because thought processes combine constituents according to specific syntactic and semantic rules that the structure of thought satisfies the Generality Constraint. As we will see, visual processes combine primitive constituents according to their spatial locations but not according to a formal grammar. For this reason, vision lacks the logical structure that is necessary to satisfy the Generality Constraint. Hence, it lacks the properties that are necessary for a system to be systematic.

In contrast with these arguments, I am going to show that visual representations, like conceptual representations, have a structure of constituents, and so that the visual representation system is systematic, even though vision structurally differs from higher-cognition.

4.3 Systematicity of Binding Operations in Vision

Visual binding operations are a prime example of structured processes in vision: Binding requires the combination of primitive features for creating an object representation. Is this combination performed in a systematic way? In other words, do early and mid-level visual processes have a structure of constituency? In order to address this question, I am going first to present already existing accounts of the systematicity of vision in structural models of object recognition (Biederman, 1987; Hummel and Biederman, 1992; Hummel, 2001). Then, I will propose my account of systematicity, based on psychophysical and neurophysiological findings that explain binding in terms of attentional control and synchronization mechanisms.

4.3.1 *The alleged systematicity of structural models of object recognition*

Models of object recognition exhibit a systematic behavior in the way primitive components are combined. The clearest examples are models based on Biederman's Recognition by Components theory (Hummel and Biederman, 1992; Hummel, 2001). According to this theory, object recognition depends on the combination of primitive volumetric features according to particular categorical relations. Among those, spatial relations between object's parts provide critical constraints for the construction of an object representation. For example, if a curved cylinder were attached on the top of a straight cylinder, then we would have a representation of a bucket, but if the curved cylinder were attached instead on the right side of the straight cylinder, then the resulting representation would be that of a cup. The overall structure of those object representations can be represented by a syntactic tree, in which the different primitive parts are the leaves of the tree connected to a superior node that represents the spatial relation among the primitives. The resulting representation is equivalent to the structure of thoughts as defined in propositional accounts, and the resulting process is classically systematic and compositional. But its systematicity and compositionality come at the price of having language-like processes in vision. In fact, structural models of object recognition reduce the spatial and parallel-distributed architecture of vision to a hierarchical tree in which spatial representations are represented in a language-like fashion, as extrinsic to the visual architecture. Additionally, structural models perform *ad hoc* computations, so that the resulting properties match the background theory. Those models are thus far from being biologically plausible models of visual object representations.

A different way to account for visual binding and the role of spatial relations has been proposed (Edelman and Intrator, 2003). According to this view, the systematicity of visual feature binding can be explained without committing to a propositional account of visual processes:

An alternative, non-classical approach to systematicity is to represent an object by a set of non-categorical, non-generic measurements that are somehow spatially structured. We propose to use location in the visual field in lieu of the abstract frame that encodes object structure. Intuitively, the constituents of an object are then bound to each other by virtue of residing in their proper places in the visual field [...]. The visual field can then be thought of as a corkboard, whose spatial structure supports the arrangement of shape fragments pinned to it [...]. This scheme exhibits effective systematicity by virtue of its ability to represent different arrangements of the same constituents [...]. (Edelman and Intrator, 2003, pp. 78–79, *italics SE and NI*).

Edelman and Intrator point out that the structure of vision does not need to perfectly match the structure of higher cognitive processes in order to have a combinatorial structure of representations. They propose a way to consider systematicity in vision by highlighting the role of the topographic feature maps in representing spatial information. This solution does not involve the explicit representation of spatial relations among features and objects.[6] My analysis of visual feature binding as accomplished by dynamic mechanisms (attention and temporal synchrony) is consistent with Edelman and Intrator's approach, even if they postulate a static model of binding. Thus, I will claim that visual feature binding has a structure of constituents, even if spatial relations among features and objects are not explicitly represented.

4.3.2 *Visual feature binding (first-order binding)*

The hypotheses of binding by attention and synchrony are not mutually exclusive. Binding by attention provides a functional explanation of feature binding; whereas binding by synchrony explains how binding can be implemented at a neuronal level (Crick and Koch, 1990; Treisman, 1996). In fact, as described in chapter three, studies of 'illusory conjunctions' and visual search support the role of spatial attention in binding features occupying the same location, and neurophysiological findings support the idea that the focus of attention on a particular location enhances the synchrony of the activity of neurons coding for stimulus' features at the selected location. Synchronous neuronal activity is thought to gate information to subsequent stages of the visual process, and has been related to two further operations in vision that might complement the process of binding in recovering object representation: (1) Synchrony is thought to be the active mechanism underlying the binding of a feature across space (von der Malsburg, 1981); that is, the pre-attentive grouping of the same feature occurring at different location but belonging to the same object; and (2) synchrony of neuronal activity might be involved in storing integrated representations of objects in visual working memory (Luck and Vogel, 1997).

---

[6] Whether spatial relations among objects are explicitly or implicitly represented in the visual system is a matter of debate in vision science (Tarr and Bülthoff, 1998).

Does feature binding as accomplished by attention and synchrony have a structure of causally connected constituents? To address this, I will consider the logical character of visual feature binding. If binding is achieved dynamically, then visual feature binding is a systematic process.

Generally, the binding process, in the case of a visual scene in which a green-horizontal bar and a red-vertical bar are presented, can be schematized as follows:

(*i*)   (green and horizontal) (red and vertical)

In order to represent (*i*), feature conjunctions need to be grouped according to the object they belong to. To this extent, something additional to conjunction is needed for the grouping. In fact, if (*i*) is represented only by means of conjoining the presented features, then there is no way to discriminate features that belong to an object. For example, there is no difference between a scene representing (green and horizontal and red and vertical) and a scene representing (red and horizontal and green and vertical): Both scenes involve the discrimination of four features but this discrimination does not allow distinguishing between the two scenes. In order to properly combine features and discriminate the two bars described in (*i*), one has to detect (*i*) as containing representations of two objects. For this reason, it has been argued that feature binding requires identity (Clark, 2000; Cohen, 2004a; Werning, 2005). That is to say, features must be perceived as predicates of the same entity. The process of binding, then, can be schematized as follows (Clark, 2000):

(*ii*) a is F
          b is G
          ───────────────
          Something is both F and G

Where F and G correspond to the value of the features in two separate feature maps, and 'a' and 'b' are the entity to which features are attributed. In the case of (*i*), F and G correspond to green and horizontal ((*ii*) simplifies matter by reporting the binding of features belonging to one object; see below for a complete schema). According to the feature integration theory of attention, spatial attention is the mechanism that actively binds all features occupying the same location (Treisman and Gelade, 1980). In this framework, attention selecting the same location is the 'glue' that secures identity. Thus, 'a' and 'b' are taken to be spatial locations. If we substitute 'a' and 'b' with the location in which features occur, then the schema in (*ii*) turns to be:

(*iii*)   At loc_i is F
          At loc_j is G
          ───────────────
          At loc_i is both F and G

The role of attention is to secure identification: It determines when features have a common subject matter and allows the identification and discrimination of different objects. The common object matter is location, at least at the level of binding of features occurring at the same location by spatial attention. On this basis, Clark (2000) argues that the reference of sensory identification is location; resulting in the controversial claim that sensory experience is *about* location. This position has been criticized based on the evidence for object-based attention selecting bound representations (e. g., Blaser *et al.* 2000). Evidence for object-based attention argues for sensory identity as being secured by objects identification (Cohen, 2004a; Matthen, 2004). I am leaving the issue about sense and reference to a later part of the chapter. For the moment, I consider *(iii)* as a good description of binding of features at the same location by spatial attention, and will endorse its consequences for some more pages.

The logical characterization of visual binding across feature dimensions, as reported in *(ii)* and *(iii)*, has the advantage to outline the structure of the binding operations. This structure resembles the structure of thought as defined in Evans' Generality Constraint. In order to evaluate whether visual binding operations satisfy the requirements of the Generality Constraint, one needs to investigate whether the primitive features combined in one object representation are the same as the ones combined in a structural related representation of another object sharing several features with the first object. Moreover, one needs to consider whether visual features contribute in the same way, during the binding processes of structurally related object, to determine the structure of the complex objects of which they are primitive constituents. If it turns out to be the case, then one can conclude that visual feature binding has a structure of constituency, and, as such, is systematic.

Let us consider a simple scene with two objects: A green-horizontal bar and a red-vertical bar. Positing this simple scenario is required by the fact that the binding problem in vision emerges only in the presence of multiple objects; that is, in the case of visual scenes. The chosen example is, then, the simplest possible scene that requires binding across feature dimensions. To represent this scene, one needs an expanded version of *(ii)*:

$(iv.a)$ a is F c is H
          b is G d is M
          $a = b$ $c = d$
          ─────────────────────   ─────────────────────
          Something is both F and G Something is both H and M

          a,b,c,d = location in the feature maps[7]
          F   = green   ⎫
          G   = horizontal ⎬ features values
          H   = red   ⎮
          M   = vertical ⎭

───────────

[7] To be more precise, 'a', 'b', 'c', and 'd' represent objects locations in the saliency map, which point to the corresponding locations in the feature maps (see, for example, fig. 3.4 in ch. 3).

A recombination of the primitive visual constituents in *(iv.a)* that structurally satisfies the Generality Constraint requires that at least one of the four features changes its position. A visual scene containing, for example, a green-vertical bar and a red-horizontal bar would do the purpose:

(iv.b) a is F c is H

b is M d is G

$\underline{a = b}$ $\underline{c = d}$

Something is both F and M Something is both H and G

a,b,c,d = location in the feature maps

F   = green   ⎫
G   = horizontal ⎬ features values
H   = red   ⎭
M   = vertical

The same applies to any other possible recombination of features, in which the extreme option is that the recombination of features is as such that all the features are shifted, so that the two discriminable objects result to be the same objects but in different locations.

The above configurations show how visual features might be recombined in a systematic way by means of combining predicates (features) in a formal language. Vision combines its primitive constituents according to their location; failing to implement the language-like processes that underlie the structure of constituents in thought. To this extent, I investigate whether neuronal processes implement something similar to *(iv.a/b)*. If neuronal processes underlying feature binding across dimensions turn to have this structure, then visual feature binding is a systematic process.

Neuroscientific studies support the claim that when two instantiations of the same feature occur at different locations, the same feature map (coding for that particular feature) is active; but the activations within this feature map are distinct, corresponding to the two distinct feature locations. In the particular case of *(iv.a)* and *(iv.b)* the same feature maps representing green, red, vertical, and horizontal are active. Differences between the two configurations are represented by changes in the features' locations as represented in the feature maps. Then, attention selects object locations and thereby combines features so that from the binding of features in *(iv.a)* and *(iv.b)* different representations result. Thus, *(iv.a)* and *(iv.b)* can be respectively represented as:

(*iv.c*) At loc_i is F At loc_m is H
      At loc_j is G At loc_g is M
      $\underline{\text{loc}_i = \text{loc}_j}$ $\underline{\text{loc}_m = \text{loc}_g}$
      At loc_i is both F and G At loc_m is both H and M

(*iv.d*) At loc_i is F At loc_m is H
      At loc_j is M At loc_g is G
      $\underline{\text{loc}_i = \text{loc}_j}$ $\underline{\text{loc}_m = \text{loc}_g}$
      At loc_i is both F and M At loc_m is both H and G

The process of feature binding turns to be more than simple input-output association: Binding is as such that whenever features occupying the same location are selected, their combination is represented. In this process, primitive constituents are tokened simultaneously with the complex representation, so that lacking one of the constituents will result in the failure of binding. Moreover, The focus of attention on specific feature detectors enhances the synchrony of neuronal activity, as shown by Fries and colleagues (2001) in area V4 of monkey. Synchronization of neuronal activity might be instrumental in the gating of feature representations to object recognition, and, thus, feature integration.

4.3.3 *The representation of extended object: Perceptual grouping*

The visual scenes so far presented reflect the stimuli used in the studies of visual feature binding. The simplicity of such scenes derives from the need to minimize the parameters to control during an experiment. For this reason, the bars presented so far fall within the receptive fields of single feature detectors and, thus, require the activation of these detectors in different feature maps. Nevertheless, real objects occupy extended regions of the visual field, requiring the activation of a larger amount of feature detectors within the same feature map. As an example, consider a simple visual scene with a red apple. The representation of the apple activates a large portion of the feature maps, for example, for color and orientation.[8] The representation of extended objects, such as the apple, posits the problem of how features represented in different regions of the same feature map are bound together. In other words, the representation of extended objects posits the question of how perceptual grouping occurs. Binding of features across space (perceptual grouping) cannot be explained by referring to spatial attention, since spatial attention locally binds features. That is to say, spatial attention binds features across dimensions (feature maps) but does not bind features across regions in the same feature map. As first pointed out by Gestalt psychologists, objects

---

[8] To simplify matter, I only consider color and orientation without entering the details of how many feature maps might be necessary to represent the actual contour of an apple.

are grouped according to specific rules (Koffka, 1935; Wertheimer, 1938; Kanisza, 1979), which might be learned through experience (Gilbert and Sigman, 2007). The hypothesis of binding by synchrony was brought up to explain how neuronal processes might implement perceptual grouping (von der Malsburg, 1981; Singer, 1999). According to it, the repetition of stable patterns in the visual world might strengthen connections among neurons involved in the representation of such configurations and thereby increase the chance that their activities synchronize. A structural model of object recognition, will describe feature grouping as (feature$_1$ collinear to feature$_2$ collinear to feature$_3$ ... collinear to feature$_n$), and represent it in a way that fits a syntactic tree, with spatial relations explicitly represented in a superior node that links together the primitive features. Instead, our account describes perceptual grouping by considering the synchrony of neuronal activity and the subsequent role of attention to integrate bound features across different feature maps. None of these two mechanisms requires that spatial relations between features be explicitly represented. Specifically, the representation of feature locations by topographic feature maps is sufficient to explain perceptual grouping and the subsequent feature binding across dimension.

Following *(ii)*, the logic behind feature grouping achieved by the synchrony of neuronal activity can be schematized as follows (Werning, 2003, 2005):

(*v*)   This is F and That is G
$$\frac{\text{This} = \text{That}}{\text{Something is both } F \text{ and } G}$$

As one can derive from the comparison of *(iii)* and *(v)*, binding by synchrony and binding by attention are structurally similar and, for what presented above, systematic.[9] However, in the case of binding by synchrony, the entities that disambiguate between object representations cannot be taken to be spatial locations. In fact, in perceptual grouping, the values of features remain the same, while location changes across individuals. Because of that, reference to location, as described by the feature integration theory of attention, is replaced with reference to the group of features (or an object).

The role of synchrony is to group the same feature across space into the representation of an object. On this basis, *(v)* can be schematized as follows:

(*v.a*) (This is F_0 and This is F_1, ..., and This F_n) and (That is G_0 and That is G_1, ..., and That is G_n)

Where the indexes indicate the different locations where feature values for orientation and color occur. This recalls Peacocke's suggestion that the representational

---

[9] For a formal account of the systematicity and compositionality of binding by synchrony, see Werning (2005).

content of sense experience has a spatial type. This spatial type is indicated by the indexes and reflects the information about location represented in the feature maps.

Recently, Wolfe (1998; Wolfe and Bennett, 1997) suggests that early perceptual grouping corresponds to features as being loosely grouped in *bundles*, as opposed to what originally theorized by feature integration theories of binding. The selection of attention to specific locations in the bundle or to the entire group of features might strengthen the connections among the features in the bundle. The latter interpretation is consistent with empirical findings related to object-based attention. However, it is not clear whether it is the selection of spatial attention to a particular location rather than the object-based selection of the bundle that enhances feature binding. Let us suppose that a space-based selection mechanism underlies feature binding, and that feature bundles are made of different detectors within the same feature map. The attentional selection of specific locations in such perceptual groups (i.e., feature bundles) might then, by virtue of the connections among the features of the bundle, spread across the entire bundle. As a result, the entire bundle, and not just the originally selected location, will be attended.

The proposed account is consistent with saying that the process leading to object representation has two components: (1) a saliency-based attentional control mechanism; and (2) a synchronization mechanism for feature grouping and integration, which results from the direction of attention. The overall process eventually terminates with the representation of an integrated object.

4.3.4 *The representation of spatial relations between objects (second-order binding)*

The relevance of storing information about location becomes evident as soon as we consider the perception of objects in a cluttered visual scene. We normally perceive objects not only as being located in a specific region but also as being related to each other. Second-order binding is about how relations, specifically spatial relations, between objects are represented by the visual system. Second-order binding in language-like processes is the representation of the states of affairs *aRb* and *bRa*, in which the constituents 'a' and 'b' are related according to a double-place relation: For example, the constituents of the thought that John loves Mary are bound to their role to the relation loves so that 'John' and 'Mary' play different causal roles in ((John)$_{NP}$ [(loves)$_V$ (Mary)$_{NP}$]$_{VP}$)$_S$ (*aRb*) and ((Mary)$_{NP}$ [(loves)$_V$ (John)$_{NP}$]$_{VP}$)$_S$ (*bRa*). A visual counterpart of second-order binding would be, for example, a scene in which there is a red apple to the left of a brown basket (*aRb*) and a brown basket to the left of a red apple (*bRa*), as shown in fig. 4.1. How are spatial relations between objects represented in vision? Is second-order binding systematic?

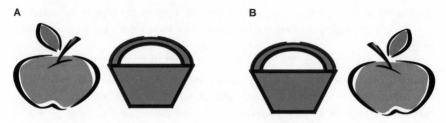

Fig. 4.1: (A) and (B) respectively represent a visual scene with a red apple to the left of a brown basket, and a visual scene with a brown basket to the left of a red apple. Note that, whilst objects are explicitly represented, the representation of the spatial relations between them has to be inferred from the objects' locations.

Before going into the details of second-order binding, it is necessary to make a brief digression and distinguish between explicit and implicit representations (see also Crick and Koch, 1995). An explicit representation is a representation that can be immediately decoded. For example, spatial information represented within the topographic feature maps is explicitly represented. Instead, implicit representations require further processing to be decoded. This information might be used at different stages within the same system or be ready to be decoded by other systems that receive that particular information as an input.[10] An example of implicit representation in vision would be, for example, the representation of an object in the retina: Even if the retina represents contrast and light information that is necessary for object representation, the explicit representation of an object occurs only at a later stage of the visual process. In this sense, the retina implicitly represents information about objects that need to be further processed to become explicit. A similar distinction between explicit and implicit representations can be found in Fodor (1975). Fodor distinguishes between explicit and implicit beliefs represented in the so-called 'belief-box' (Schiffer, 1981): Explicit beliefs are the ones stored within the belief box and directly available; instead, implicit beliefs result from further computational operations (such as inference) on explicit beliefs. Implicit beliefs are the resulting outputs of the performed operations, and they are not explicitly represented in the belief-box. Fodor's distinction between explicit and implicit beliefs was supposed to account for the computational burden that the explicit storage of all possible beliefs would require.

I argue that spatial relations between objects are implicitly represented in the visual system. Specifically, the visual system explicitly represents information about object locations but implicitly represents spatial relations between objects

---

[10] Heck (2007, pp. 128–133) also distinguishes between implicit and explicit representations in vision, in order to determine whether vision has a non-conceptual content. His distinction between explicit and implicit is "one between the input to computational processes and the output of them." I prefer to define the distinction in terms of what it is directly decoded and what needs further processing to become explicit, since both kinds of information can be input and output of the same processes.

like, for example, 'to the left of', 'on top of', etc. Information about spatial relations might be explicitly decoded by other systems that receive inputs from the visual system. Specifically, the 'language-system' and the 'sensory-motor system' might explicitly use visual information about object locations to describe visual scenes and for planning actions. In fact, we are able to describe fig. 4.1 as depicting an apple to the left of the basket and a basket to the left of an apple, and in the case of a real scene in which we could need to walk between the apple and the basket, our sensory-motor system coordinates our movements so that we can easily pass in between the two objects.

According to this theoretical assumption, that is consistent with feature hier-archy models (e.g., Edelman and Intrator, 2003), the visual system explicitly represents the locations of objects in the saliency maps. Thus, the two objects in fig.4.1 are represented in two distinct positions, and, according to the provided description of feature binding, this process might be implemented by exploiting the topographic organization of visual feature maps (fig. 4.2). I also argued that a process is systematic if it can deal with various spatial arrangements of the same constituents. Since the apple and the basket are represented according to their locations, then second-order binding is also systematic. However, the spatial relation between the two objects is probably implicitly represented in vision. For this reason, the representation of spatial relations between objects in vision dif-fers from the representation of the two-place relations in language-like processes, such as thought and the structural models of visual object recognition, since these processes explicitly represent relations between constituents (Hayworth *et al.*, 2008).

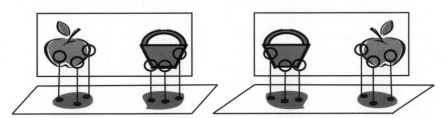

Fig. 4.2: The representation of structurally related visual scenes depends on the activation of objects' locations in the saliency maps. The explicit representation of objects' locations is necessary to properly bind features and, thus, represent coherent objects. Nevertheless, the representation of spatial relations between objects, such as, for example, the spatial relation between the apple and the basket, is probably not explicitly represented in the visual system (adapted from Edelman and Intrator, 2003).

To recapitulate: I argue that second-order binding is systematic and its systematicity can be explained by referring to the structure of first-order binding (visual feature binding). Spatial relations between objects are probably implicitly represented at early visual stages, and decoded either at later stages of the visual processing or by other systems. My argument is based on purely theoretical assumptions, because of the lack of conclusive evidence for how these kinds of relations are implemented by brain processes.[11]

Nevertheless, on the basis of what presented so far, it is possible to argue that visual short-term memory probably plays a role in the recovery of information necessary for representing spatial relations. Attention – considered to be the mechanism underlying the representation of an object at a particular location – serially scans visual scenes, so that only one object can be attended at once. In order to represent spatial relations between objects (second-order binding), objects' representations need to be retained in memory. This step is necessary to compare objects' positions and compute their relations. It has been theorized that synchrony might play a role in retaining object representations in visual short-term memory (Luck and Vogel, 1997). If this is the case, then feature integration by attention (and the pre-attentive perceptual grouping) and visual short-term memory together provide all the information necessary for identifying objects and their locations, that eventually turns in the explicitly representation of spatial relations.

4.3.5 *Differences between the structure of vision and the structure of cognition*

I have so far characterized feature binding in terms of its logical properties and how these properties might be related to neuronal processes underlying binding. The risk of this kind of analysis is to confuse the levels of explanation: There is nothing that it is language-like in binding per se, even if its operations can be formalized by means of conjunction and identity. From this formalization certain properties derive: Vision has a structure of constituents and binding processes are systematic. However, the architecture of visual feature binding is not similar to a formal grammar. Consider for example the operations that might be implemented by vision. Visual feature binding requires the integration and grouping of primitive features. To this extent, operations as conjunction and identity are required. Nonetheless, it is not possible to characterize any of the processes involved in binding in terms of other logical operations. Consider, for example, negation and disjunction: There is no feature integration that is the negation of any of the integrations that occur within the visual system, and even though feature conjunction is a well studied process, feature disjunction does not exist; either features are conjoint or there are not combined at all.[12] Then, it follows that vision does not possess the rich propositional structure that higher-cognitive processes seems to have.

However, it is important to point out that, notwithstanding that vision lacks a language-like structure of constituents, vision does not fail to implement such

---

[11] For an alternative account of second-order binding, see Werning (2003).

[12] A useful table that describes the distinction between language-like and visual processes can be found in Kosslyn *et al.* (2006).

a structure. Language-like architecture implements the causal role of the constituents, according to the order in which the constituents are tokened. Instead, the causal role of the constituents is determined in vision by their spatial location. Thus, space is the relation of order that determines the role of the constituents in the construction of a complex representation.

4.4 Sense and Reference

Finally, I would like to address the issue of sensory reference that has been in the air since a while. I take sensory reference to be a basic form of reference in which a person can perceive an object and, in virtue of her perception, can also point to it. The perception of an object per se does not seem to be sufficient to secure reference: If one wants to refer to a particular object than she needs to attend to it. Thus, attention and reference seem to be related phenomena (Campbell, 2004). How does sensory reference relate to the explanation of visual feature binding?

For what I presented so far, two operations are required in order to secure feature binding: *(i)* the extraction of features; and *(ii)* their integration. The selection of specific entities to which features are predicated secures reference; that is to say, it allows for the disambiguation between objects. As Clark puts it:

> To get to identity statements we need to add a new *kind* of term, with a distinct function. These are singular terms, names or terms like names, that are used to identify. So if feature integration works as these models propose, then within sentience itself we find capacities that fill two distinct logical functions. One is proto-predicative: the capacity to sense red both here and there. The other is proto-referential: the capacity to identify the red region as one that is also stippled. This is an informative identity grasped sub-personally. (Clark, 2004a, p. 450).

According to Clark, regions in space-time secures object identity but, as he admits, this conception can be criticized based on the perception of motion over time:

> Motion perception provides a prima facie counter-example to the thesis that sensory individuals are space-time regions. After all, one defining characteristic of a space-time region is that it does not move. Its occupants might, but it cannot. So if one perceives something to move, one must (it seems) be perceiving individuals other than space-time regions. (Clark, 2004b, p. 557).

Therefore, sensory reference must be to object and not location. The idea that sensory individuals are objects is supported by studies of object-based attention in multiple object tracking (MOT) experiments (Pylyshyn and Storm, 1988). To briefly recapitulate, during MOT subjects are asked to track up to five random moving targets on a screen. According to Pylyshyn and colleagues, the ability to successfully track the targets accounts for an object-based primitive mechanism in early vision that selects and maintains the identity of individual objects. Pylyshyn

(2007) argues that this primitive mechanism (FINST) points to, or indexes, the target, and that the index assigned to the target sticks to its referent (the target) as it moves. Because of the indexing of targets, a subject is then able to keep track of the targets that are randomly moving. Proponents of FINST theory consider visual sensory individuals to be objects. Which kind of objects? As Pylyshyn (2001) notices, objects selected by visual indexes are not the three dimensional objects of our visual experience. Instead, they are *proto-object*: "[...] clusters of proximal features that serve as precursor in the detection of real physical objects (Pylyshyn, 2001, p. 144, *fn. 5*)." A proto-object is, thus, something more than the simple features described in Feature Integration Theory, and yet it is not a full 3D object.

Thus, there are at least two ways to consider what sensory individuals are: Sensory identification refers to location in the frame of spatial attention, and objects in the frame of object-based attention. My intuition is that it might be redundant to have different theories of reference for each level of the hierarchy of object recognition. If (and only if) something similar to reference occurs in vision, then it occurs only at a later visual stage, where objects are actually represented. Early visual processes involved in feature binding secure integration but reference is about the object resulting from this integration. In this work, I considered the implementation of the role of attention by means of synchrony. Synchrony underlies the perceptual grouping of features across space, resulting in the representation of an object. This view is quite sympathetic with the idea that sensory identification is secured by relating features to a specific object.

However, this is not satisfactory yet. The idea that sensory reference is about object might be misleading. If one considers the final product of our visual perception, one can easily say that it involves information about objects and their locations. Sensory processes involved in visual feature binding explicitly represent both feature values and their location: At an early stage of the process, the identity of location secures feature integration that it is subsequently processed as an integrated object throughout the entire visual architecture. However, in order to represent spatial relations between objects, information about multiple object locations has to be simultaneously stored. If the hypothesis that the synchronous activity of neurons might allow for storing such information is correct, then reference is about object and also involves a *spatial type* for representing the ways objects are located. At this point an explanation of how information about spatial relations is finally rendered explicit in the phenomenal perception of a visual scene is still missing. But this depends more on the outcomes of empirical studies of visual scene perception, than on my theoretical analysis. However, I think that, because of the characteristic of the visual system, sensory reference cannot be detached from being about an object at a specific location.

4.5 Conclusion

I argued for the systematicity of visual feature binding as accomplished by attentive and synchronous mechanisms. This approach extends already existing theoretical studies of the structure of visual binding operations. I stressed the role of space-based attention as an active binding mechanism, based on psychological and neuroscientific findings. Following Clark (2000), I defined the logical properties of feature binding. Nevertheless, my approach diverges from Clark's for the following:

> I was distressed to be read as being opposed to "Intentionalism", for I certainly do think that sensory states are intentional states, that they have a content, that they are more or less veridical, that they can be evaluated semantically; indeed that they have something like a subject-predicate structure, *though they are not sentential and do not manifest most of the hallmarks of compositionality.* (Clark, 2004b, p. 571; *italics MCT*).

As I hope to have shown, the fact that the visual structure is not sentential does not involve lack of systematicity (and compositionality). The process of visual feature binding depends on the combination of visual primitive features according to a structure of constituency, in which features are the actual constituents of the object representation, opposite to a simple input-output association. The systematicity of visual feature binding derives from how visual features are combined by means of attentional and synchronous mechanisms and from the representation of spatial information by means of topographic feature maps.

I propose that my model might also account for the (implicit) representation of the spatial relations between objects in vision. In this case, the proposed model can also account for the *massiveness* of the binding problem (Jackendoff, 2002). The massiveness of the binding problem relates to the difficulties to explain hierarchically structured relations, such as, for example, 'John loves Mary' and the perception of an apple to the left of a basket, respectively in language and vision.[13] I suggest that the implicit representation of spatial relations by means of the topographic organization of feature maps can also describe how hierarchical relations are implemented.

To conclude: I argue that the representational processes underlying visual binding are systematic. Thus, visual representations, like conceptual representations, have a structure of constituents even though vision does not have a language-like structure. From this it follows that systematicity does not only depend on formal combinatorial processes on symbolic representations but it is also a pervasive property of combinatorial and topographical structure imposed on non-conceptual representations.

---

[13] Theoretical accounts that support the role of synchrony to implement hierarchically structured relations have been proposed (see, for example, Werning, 2003).

5
Compositional Constituent
Structure in Vision

The principle of semantic compositionality is often considered a fundamental principle of semantics (Peregrin, 2005). According to this principle, the meaning of a complex expression derives from the meaning of its constituents and its structure. Furthermore, compositionality defines the requirements that a semantic theory has to meet in order to be a proper theory of meaning (Fodor, 1998b; Szabó, 2000).

Nevertheless, it is worth to immediately clarify that this chapter is *not* about the principle of semantic compositionality of the expressions in a natural language. In fact, my aim is *not* to evaluate how, for example, from the perception of a scene with a red apple, a person can utter 'Pass me that red apple', and how the meaning of this sentence depends on the meaning of its constituents. In other words, I am not proposing an alternative view of the principle of compositionality of language (Szabó, 2000). My aim *is*, instead, to evaluate whether the content of a visual object representation depends on the content of the primitive visual features that constitute it, namely, to evaluate whether vision has a compositional structure of constituents. In order to do so, I will first consider the argument for the compositionality of mental representations (Fodor and Pylyshyn, 1988): Mental representations *compose* in a way such that complex representations inherit their content from the content of (and the structure imposed on) their constituents. The principle of compositionality of mental representations has the same form of the principle of compositionality of language but, instead of focusing on the meaning of words and expressions in a natural language, it defines how the content of inner mental representations is acquired.

The reason why the same principle applies for inner mental representations and language is due to the view in philosophy of mind that thoughts have a language-like structure. On the one hand, the structure of thought mirrors the structure of natural language, so that whatever property a language has, this property is going to be a property of thought, too (Dummett, 1981). On the other hand, language expresses thoughts, so that whatever property a language has, this property roughly mirrors a property underlying the structure of thought (Evans, 1982; Fodor, 2001). It follows that mental representations have a language-like structure[1]

---

[1] Here is a way to put the issue: "It may strike you that mental representation is a lot like language, according to my version of RTM. Quite so; how could language express thought if that were not the case?" (Fodor, 1998a, p. 25. Note: RTM = Representational Theory of Mind).

and express the propositions that are the objects of our propositional attitudes (e.g., I believe that the apple is red).[2]

Since 'thought' can be considered as a synonymous term for 'mental representation' (see, for example, Fodor, 1998a, p. 25), from now on I am going to talk of the 'compositionality of thought' instead of the 'compositionality of mental representations'. This distinction is necessary because it is an open question whether the principle of compositionality applies to mental representations other than conceptual mental representations. That is to say, it is an open question whether non-conceptual mental representations have a compositional structure of constituents. To show that vision, as a non-conceptual representational system, is compositional is the aim of this chapter. Specifically, I will argue that among the varieties of the principle of compositionality at our disposal, the principle of syntactic compositionality – a *deflationary* view of the role of compositionality in constraining semantic theories (see chapter two, and Horwich, 1998) – is the one that explains how visual representations compose.

5.1 Compositionality and Its Relation to Systematicity

The principle of compositionality of thought has a prominent role in explaining why thoughts are systematic. In fact, "[…] which sentences are systematically related is not arbitrary from a semantic point of view (Fodor and Pylyshyn, 1988, p. 41)." In order for a subject to be able to entertain systematic related thoughts, such as the thoughts that aRb and bRa, the representations aRb and bRa need to have the same constituents. Only if the constituents contribute with the same content into the determination of the content of the complex thought, then a subject can think, for example, that John loves Mary (aRb) and Mary loves John (bRa). Systematicity requires the ability of a subject to *represent as* (McLaughlin, 2009): It is because a subject grasps, for example, the concepts JOHN and MARY that she can use them in different thoughts. But it does not follow that if one is able to think about Mary, then she can also think Mary likes flowers unless, she possesses the concept FLOWER. Thus, a semantic combinatorial structure is necessary to explain systematicity: There cannot be a system that has a systematic combinatorial structure but it is not compositional.

---

[2] It is a matter of controversy whether mental representations have a language-like structure. It has been argued that mental representations can have different formats: (1) Visual representations have a pictorial format as opposed to the descriptive format of the representations involved in thought processes (Kosslyn, 1994), (2) Mental representations are sub-symbols, namely, the result of the activity in a connectionist network (Smolensky, 1988). It does not matter for the purpose of this work to define the format of mental representations, so that I leave open which of these formats is the one used in cognitive processes.

The relation between compositionality and systematicity is also necessary to avoid compositionality to be a vacuous principle. It has been demonstrated that the principle of compositionality without syntactic and semantic constraints turns to be vacuous; that is to say, the principle of compositionality, defined as a function that assigns meanings to terms, cannot exclude any kind of meaning, since any arbitrary meaning assignment can be compositional (Zadrozny, 1994). Two minimal constraints for a system to be compositional are:

(1) The content of a representation is derived from the content of the constituents in a systematic way.

(2) The content of the constituents is primitive.

These constraints imply that for a system to be compositional a structure of primitive constituents, which can systematically combine is required. As Fodor suggests:

> Since the argument that concepts compose is primarily that they are productive and systematic, we can simply stipulate that the claim that concepts compose is true only if the syntax and content of complex concepts is derived from the syntax and content of their constituents *in a way that explains their productivity and systematicity*. (Fodor, 1998a, p. 94; *italics JAF*).

In the previous chapter, I have shown that visual binding processes underlying visual object representation are systematic, and, thus, that visual representations have a structure of constituents. Since systematicity depends on compositionality, and to the extent that visual binding processes are systematic, then they must be compositional, too.

5.2 Compositionality of Visual Representations[3]

Let us assume that visual representations, like conceptual representations, *compose*, so that the content of an object representation depends on the content of its primitive constituents and their structure. In other words, let us assume that vision is compositional. In order to prove the validity of such an assumption, it is necessary *(i)* to evaluate whether visual primitive constituents play the same role in determining the content of a visual object (and as an extension of a visual scene); and *(ii)* to account for the application of the principle of compositionality to non-conceptual representations.

---

[3] Here, I will only focus on the systematicity argument for compositionality. As motivated in chapter two, I consider the visual system to be a finite representational system that lacks the recursive capacity for being productive. Nevertheless, even if finite representational systems, such as vision, fail to be productive, systematicity is a property that these systems have *qua* finite representational systems.

5.2.1 *Compositional structure of constituents*

According to Fodor, the assumption that visual representations have a compositional semantics can be so defined:

> *Picture Principle:* If P is a picture of X, then parts of P are pictures of parts of X. (Fodor, 2007, p. 108.)

In other words, visual representations are made of distinct parts, none of which is a proper constituent. To be a proper constituent, parts need to be recognized as the *canonical decomposition* of a representation (Fodor, 2007, p. 108). For example, the constituents of the thought that John loves Mary are 'John', 'Mary', and 'loves Mary', since these constituents contribute to the content of the thought. On the contrary, any other decomposition of the same thought, such as, for example, 'John ... Mary' is not a proper constituent. In Fodor's view, visual representations cannot be canonically decomposed: Any kind of decomposition of a visual representation into its constituents makes the same contribution to the content of the representation. To make an example: The decomposition of the visual representation of a flower into (petals, stem, leaves) is as good as the decomposition (part of petal$_1$, roots, sepal, stalk). Visual representations lack a structure of proper primitive constituents, and, thus, visual representations cannot be compositional and systematic.

I might, now, take Fodor's suggestion and stop bothering about the principle of compositionality for vision. Nevertheless, what so far presented is in plain contradiction with what I have shown in chapter four, namely, that the processes underlying visual object representation are systematic, and that, the visual system, has a structure of constituents.

Visual primitive constituents are features represented in early visual cortical areas. The decomposition of a visual scene into its primitive features is as such that features belonging to different objects are differently grouped, so that every feature plays a distinct role in the determination of the content of a scene. That a scene is canonically decomposed is secured by the active role of the binding mechanism that binds feature according to the object they belong to. However, vision does not combine primitive features by applying formal rules, as thought processes do: Visual object representations result from the combination of primitive features according to their spatial relations. This might turn to be a problem, since the logical structure of the processes in conceptual systems renders explicit the contribution of each constituent to the content of the whole. I argue that it is possible to disentangle the contribution of visual constituents by referring to the spatial structure of visual representations. I will constrain our analysis to the process of visual feature binding across dimensions (i.e., the binding of different features occurring at the same location).

The representation of a visual scene with a red-vertical line and a green-horizontal line results with the activation of distinct visual feature maps, specifically coding for green, red, vertical, and horizontal. Each feature map represents a specific feature; the combination of which can be described either as (At loc$_i$ is red and vertical) and (At loc$_j$ is green and horizontal) or, by considering the representations involved, as the visual representations $\vartheta((\iota)(o))$ and $\Phi((\alpha)(\varepsilon))$ (where ϑ, Φ = locations, and ι, o, α, ε = feature values).[4] The recombination of the primitive features so that one can, for example, perceive a green-vertical line and a red-horizontal line is relevant if the representations $\vartheta((\alpha)(o))$ and $\Phi((\iota)(\varepsilon))$ signal constituents with the same content, namely, the constituents contribute with the same content notwithstanding the recombination. This occurs only if one takes visual representations to have a compositional content. That visual primitive features contribute with the same content to determine the content of the whole is demonstrated by the fact that whenever the same feature appears in a scene, the feature map coding for that specific feature is active: For example, every time red is represented, the feature map for red is active. In general, this applies to every primitive feature that is represented within the cortical feature maps.

Different combinations of the same constituents lead to novel representations that have distinct contents. For example, the content of John loves Mary is different from the content of Mary loves John. In the first case, John is the one that loves someone, while in the second case it is Mary that is in love. This difference is often explained in terms of differences in the structure of the two sentences. Particularly, as Fodor suggests:

> That's largely *because*, discursive representations being semantically and syntactically heterogeneous, their various constituents can contribute in different ways to determining the content of their hosts: singular terms contribute in one way, predicates contribute in quite another way, and logical constants in still another. But the Picture Principle says that every part of an icon contributes to its interpretation in the same way: it pictures parts of what the icon does. In consequence, icons can't express (for example) the distinction between negative propositions and affirmative ones which turns (*inter alia*) on distinctions among logical constants [...]. They can't even express predication, since that requires (*inter alia*) distinguishing terms that contribute individuals from terms that contribute sets (or properties, or whatever). (Fodor, 2007, p. 109; *italics JAF*).

I agree with Fodor that vision fails to distinguish between negative and affirmative propositions but disagree on the following issue: From the fact that vision does not have a language-like structure, it follows only that vision cannot have the same repertoire of logical interpretation that thought has, but it does not follow that the visual spatial structure does not allow to distinguish among the different roles of the constituents. Thus, if visual constituents play different roles, then they can modify the content of the distinct representations they are constituents of.

---

[4] I follow the common practice in philosophy to indicate representations by using the Greek alphabet. $\vartheta((\iota)(o))$ corresponds to the visual representation with the content 'At loc$_i$ is red and vertical', and $\Phi((\alpha)(\varepsilon))$ corresponds to the visual representation with the content 'At loc$_j$ is green and horizontal'.

There is a difference between perceiving a green-vertical line and a red-vertical line, or between perceiving two green-vertical lines at two distinct locations. This difference is explained by considering the location of the represented features. Visual feature maps represent the value of a specific feature and its location within the visual field, so that features that occur in the same location are selected by an attentional mechanism and bound together. By changing the spatial location of features, different representations arise. In fact, if a green-vertical line appears in the left quadrant of the visual field, the feature maps involved will signal the corresponding feature values in that region, and, because features representing green and vertical occur in the same location, the final representation will be a green and vertical line. But, if in the same location there is a red-vertical line, then in this case, red and vertical are combined, leading to the corresponding representation.[5] The distinction between feature value and location has been described as a difference between sensory individuals and predicates (Clark, 2004a/b). While I do not think something similar to reference occurs at this level of the visual process, it is undeniable, that location and feature value play different role in the process of feature binding across dimensions. Specifically, location is the common object matter to which feature values are related, as if being predicates. Hence, visual constituents, as conceptual constituents, have *heterogeneous* roles in determining the content of the object representation.

To summarize what so far presented: The fact that structurally related visual representations share the same constituents is indicative of the underlying compositional structure of constituents. Thus, visual constituents combine in a compositional and systematic fashion.

5.2.2 *Syntactic compositionality (I)*

The principle of compositionality in its classical formulation applies to conceptual representations, and defines what it is for a subject to possess a concept. If a subject can think *aRb* and *bRa*, then she has to possess the concepts for a and b. It follows that the principle of compositionality constrains theory of concept possession and concept individuation (Fodor, 1998a). Compositionality defines the content of a complex mental representation as being completely inherited from the content and structure of its constituents but, at the same time, the primitive constituents

---

[5] Objects often overlap in natural scenes. In this case, the features of two distinct objects occupy the same location. Object overlap is a notoriously difficult case for models of object recognition. A recent study considers the relation between figure-ground segregation and attention, with interesting results for the topic of overlapping figures (Kastner and McMains, 2007; Qiu *et al.*, 2007): Figures are segmented into likely objects throughout the visual system, and this segmentation provides information for attentional selection. This segregation allows assigning different borders to objects that overlap.

have to contribute with *all* their content to the determination of the content of the complex mental representation (Fodor, 2001). For example, if the content of the primitive representations is their inferential role (or a prototype, a recognitional concept, and so on), then the content of the complex mental representation, built up from the combination of those constituents, is its inferential role (or a prototype, a recognitional concept, and so on). The principle of compositionality rules out some of the available theories of meaning by evaluating whether the properties of the primitive representations can actually compose (Fodor, 1998b). Hence, compositionality determines the characteristics of theories of content possession for both complex and primitive mental representations.

On the contrary, the content of visual primitive representations is non-conceptual: A mental state has a non-conceptual content if and only if the subject of the state needs not to possess the concepts required to specify the content of the mental state. In order to see a red apple, a subject needs not to possess the concepts RED and APPLE; the possession of which is, instead, required to *see* the red apple *as* the red apple. Since visual representations do not require processes on conceptual primitive representations, the principle of compositionality, defined as a constraint on theories of content, is too a strong requirement for explaining the compositionality of visual representations. I proposed in chapter two a different interpretation of the principle of compositionality – the principle of syntactic compositionality – to account for the compositionality of visual representations. The principle of syntactic compositionality is defined as follows:

[CS] The content of a non-conceptual complex representation depends on the structure imposed on its constituents that have a specific content.

The principle of syntactic compositionality imposes no constraints on how the meaning properties of the constituents are constituted. Thus, this principle is neutral about which are the meaning properties of the primitive constituents, and which kinds of properties compose.

The principle of syntactic compositionality as applied to visual representations requires that *(i)* vision has a systematic structure, and that *(ii)* visual primitive constituents have a specific content. The relation between systematicity and compositionality in vision does not need further explanation. I have already argued that the fact that structurally related visual representations involve the same constituents can be explained in terms of the compositional structure of the visual constituents.

The content of primitive visual features is the information that feature maps code for. Specifically, a feature map has the content that p only if it covaries with the information that p (Drestke, 1988). One could also say that the teleological function of feature maps is to carry specific information (Millikan, 1984, 1986, 1989; Fodor, 1990): For example, a feature map represents red rather than vertical because the teleological function of that feature map is to carry the information that red. Some teleological theories account for the notion of function in terms of the evolution of a system, namely, in terms of a system's contribution to the fitness of an organism (Millikan, 1984). If we relate this notion to the structure of the visual system it equals to say: Visual feature maps (and, in general, the visual system) have the function to carry specific types of information (i.e., color, motion, orientation, etc.) because the organizing principle of feature maps emerge from natural selection. I am aware of the problems that information theories and teleological accounts of content have to face (see Cohen, 2004b, for a review) but it is hard to see how the visual system could represent information in a different way, unless one argues that vision is a non-representational system.

5.2.3 *Syntactic compositionality (II)*

The principle of syntactic compositionality of visual representations is based on Horwich's *deflationary* account of compositionality (Horwich, 1997, 2001, 2005). A deflationary account of compositionality does not involve any assumption about how the content of the primitive constituents is constituted. As a consequence, compositionality defines only how the content of a complex expression is derived from imposing a certain structure on the constituents but does not include the explanation of how constituents have that particular content. It appears that syntactic compositionality does not seem to involve anything more than it is expressed in the deflationary account.

Nevertheless, these two accounts can be distinguished by considering what they try to explain. Horwich's deflationary account is an attempt to define how sentences have a particular meaning by proposing that the structure of the sentences and the meaning of the constituents are sufficient to explain it. For example, in order to explain why the sentence 'dogs bark' means that DOGS BARK one has to explain how the sentence meaning is derived from the meaning of the words dogs and bark. In fact, given that (Horwich, 1997, pp. 505–506):

(*i*)   The meaning of 'dog' is DOG.
(*ii*) The meaning of 'bark' is BARK.
(*iii*) A sentence with the structure ⟨ns, v⟩ means ⟨NS, V⟩ (i.e., the meaning that results from applying a certain structure to the meaning of the constituents).

And

(*iv*) 'dogs bark' results from putting the words 'dog' and 'bark' into the structure ⟨ns, v⟩.

Then, it follows that:

(∴)   'dogs bark' means DOGS BARK since it results from putting the words meaning DOG and BARK in the structure meaning ⟨NS, V⟩.

The principle of syntactic compositionality, instead, explains how the content of complex non-conceptual representations is derived by the structural processes that combine together primitive features. This is where the two theories diverge: Syntactic compositionality explains how non-conceptual representations compose; whereas a deflationary account of compositionality explains how conceptual meaning compose. The deflationary view of compositionality (as a theory of meaning) has been subjected to various objections (Horwich, 1997; Fodor and Lepore, 2001), none of which seems to involve the principle of syntactic compositionality (as a theory of non-conceptual content). Among the objections, the main concern is about the vacuity of an account of compositionality that relies mostly on how constituents are combined. Compositionality, as a fundamental law of semantics, sets the boundaries of what a proper theory of meaning is supposed to require. If compositionality reduces to explain how we understand the meaning of a sentence without telling us how actually the meaning of the constituents is acquired, then that principle is vacuous. It makes a difference to state that the meaning properties of the primitives have a role in the definition of the meaning of the sentence; the difference is to have a theory of meaning for both lexical terms and sentences. The deflationary position gives only half of the explanation: It explains how the meaning property of a complex expression consists of the properties characterizing its construction, while it does not make any assumption about the underlying nature of meaning:

> As far as compositionality is concerned, the meaning property of a word could derive from its reference, an internal conceptual role, a construct out of possible worlds, some relation to a communal use, or anything else. [...] Insofar as we would like to be able to say positively what a meaning property is, it might seem that the deflationary approach to compositionality takes us in the wrong direction – by expanding rather than narrowing, the range of live options. (Horwich, 1997, pp. 531–532).

Why a fundamental law of meaning has to multiply, instead of narrowing, the possible theories of meaning? Notice that the same problem applies if the deflationary account is applied to explain the compositionality of conceptual mental representations. In fact, since being in the representational state that a is F requires the subject to be able to possess the concepts that $\underline{a}$ and $\underline{F}$, one has to explain which are the properties of the constituents inherited from the whole that contribute to its content. In general, one can assume that a deflationary account faces this problem whenever it takes into account conceptual representations (or meaningful terms in language). On the contrary, the principle of syntactic compositionality does not face the problem of vacuity, because it applies to non-conceptual representations.

A theory of content of non-conceptual mental representations appeals to the biological function of a system that carries specific information. At the level of visual representational processes, one does not need to explain how from the perception of a red object one can think about a red object, and what makes our thoughts, thoughts about that object. How conceptual representations have a particular meaning is what a semantic theory tries to explain. The visual system per se does not seem to provide anything more than *raw-representations* with a specific content that has still to be transformed into our conceptual knowledge. How this is done is an interesting question related to how non-conceptual and conceptual systems can exchange information.

5.3 Formal Details

The principle of compositionality is considered within computational cognitive science as a principle that defines how to build complex structures from simpler one by concatenation. As described above, Zadrozny (1994) demonstrated that the principle of compositionality without any further constraint is vacuous. In fact, given a set S of strings generated via concatenation from an alphabet A, a set M, and a meaning function m that assigns members of M to members of S. A function μ that maps all the element of S to M can be constructed such that:

(a) $\mu(s \cdot t) = \mu(s)(\mu(t))$ and $\mu(s)(s) = m(s)$

The outcome of the theorem is that every assignment of meaning to any expression is compositional. A way to bypass this problem is to constrain the principle of compositionality. Two minimal requirements are: *(i)* There has to be a set of primitive constituents with specific contents, and *(ii)* these constituents combine in a systematic way. Thus, compositionality holds if it explains how constituents systematically combine. If we accept these constrains, then *(a)* does not pose any challenge to the significance of compositionality (Kazmi and Pelletier, 1998; Westerståhl, 1998; Szabó, 2000; Peregrin, 2005).

Syntactic compositionality defines the content of a complex representation as depending on how its constituents are combined. Edelman and Intrator (2003) report how the syntactical recombination of visual representations fulfills the requirements for systematicity.[6] Their approach aims to explain the systematicity of second-order binding (i.e., the relation between objects in a visual scene). I briefly report their approach, and, then, apply it to the explanation of the principle of syntactic compositionality of visual feature binding (first-order binding). The

---

[6] Edelman and Intrator (2003) describe what they call semantic systematicity, namely, a way to define systematicity without presupposing the principle of compositionality. Their results show how a systematic structure imposed on visual representations with specific contents explains why the content of complex visual representations depends on the content of their constituents. This is also what the principle of syntactic compositionality explains but without denying the principle of compositionality as a basic principle underlying systematicity.

principle of syntactic compositionality (see, *fn. 7*) of second-order binding is as follows (Edelman and Intrator, 2003, *appendix a*):

Let us consider two visual objects u, $v \in U$ (sets of objects), which differ only in location ($\exists t \in T$, where T is the set of translations acting on members of U), so that $u \leftarrow^T \rightarrow v$. Let $M \subseteq M$ be a set of *measurement functions*, parameterized by location $t \in T$, so that $m: U \times T \rightarrow R$, where R is a two-place relation (e.g., on top of, to the right of, etc.). A measurement function provides the representation of a visual pattern that is present in a scene. The set of measurement functions M can support effectively systematic representations if the locations where the stimuli occur can be discriminated by means of the measurement functions, so that:

$$(*) \qquad \forall u, v \in U \text{ such that } u \leftarrow^T \rightarrow v, \exists m \in M \subseteq M : m\,(u; \cdot) \neq m\,(v; \cdot)$$

This condition defines that two objects are in two different locations. ($*$) describes the hypothesis that by explicitly representing object locations, the visual system implicitly represents their spatial relations. A systematic recombination of the configuration above involves that the two stimuli that can be distinguished at a particular location can also be distinguished when occupying a location different from the previous one:

$$(**) \qquad \exists m_i \in M : m_i\,(u; t_1) \neq (v; t_1) \Leftrightarrow \exists m_j \in M : m_j\,(u; t_2) \neq m_j\,(v; t_2)$$

This condition corresponds to the requirement that two distinct objects that are in a particular spatial relation occupy two different positions, such as, for example, that the object a is on top of the object b. ($**$) secures that the objects are two atomic representations that can be interchanged. Without this condition systematicity cannot be granted.

It is possible to derive the principle of compositionality for visual feature binding across space (first-order binding) from Edelman and Intrator's model of second-order binding. This can be done under the assumption that spatial relations between objects are implicitly represented by the visual system, and that the systematicity and compositionality of second-order binding can be derived from the structure of first-order binding. Let us add an additional clause to the ones mentioned above: That a, b, c, $d \in F \subseteq U$ denotes four features belonging to the set F of the visual primitive features. Let us suppose that a, b are constituents of the object u, and c, d are constituents of the object v (i.e., $(a \cdot b) = u$, $(c \cdot d) = v$). Then, the following represents how two features occurring at the same location are properly bound to represent an object, and how features belonging to two distinct objects occupy distinct locations:

$$(***) \qquad \forall\, a, b, c, d, \in F \text{ such that } a, b \leftarrow^T \rightarrow c, v,$$
$$\exists m_i, m_j \in M \subseteq M : (m_i\,(a; \cdot) = m_i\,(b; \cdot)) \wedge (m_j\,(c; \cdot) = m_j\,(d; \cdot)); m_i \neq m_j$$

This condition states that features occurring at the same locations are combined, and that features are combined to form two distinct object representations. It is easy to see how from this it follows that features at different locations can be recombined to form novel representations:

$$(****)\ \exists m_i \in M: m_i\ [(a;\ t_1) = (b;\ t_1)] \neq m_i\ [(c;\ t_1) = (d;\ t_1)] \Leftrightarrow \exists m_j \in M: m_j$$
$$[(a;\ t_2) = (b;\ t_2)] \neq m_j\ [(c;\ t_2) = (d;\ t_2)]$$

And, since $a \cdot b = u$ and $c \cdot d = v$, if one now substitutes u and v to S1 and S2, we obtain $(**)$, namely, the condition that guarantees the systematicity of second-order binding. What I wanted to show is that the spatial relations between objects, in early visual processing, might be nothing over and above the location of objects as already represented in visual feature binding. Since the process of visual feature binding is instrumental to object perception, the systematicity of second-order binding is derived from the systematicity of first-order binding. For reason described above, I take the systematicity of visual feature binding to reflect the underlying compositionality of the process.

5.4 On the Aboutness of Vision

For a system to be representational certain properties apply (Drestke, 1981; Bermúdez, 1995):

(i) It allows for misrepresentation: A representational system can wrongly represent the world, namely, it can represent states of affairs that differ from what is actually in the world.

(ii) It is compositionally structured: Complex representations have primitive representations as parts.

(iii) It admits of cognitive integration: The matching of represented information with previous stored information.[7]

Both thought and the visual system satisfy *(i)*, *(ii)*, and *(iii)*. For example, we can misrepresent events in the world by entertaining false beliefs, such as the belief that today is the first day of spring, when actually it is not. As described in LOT, to be in a belief state is to be in a relation with a mental representation that expresses the content of the belief (Fodor, 1975). Particularly, mental representations are structured, so that the content of a belief depends on the combination of atomic mental representations that correspond to the proposition expressed in the belief (Fodor, 1975). The content of visual perception can also be true or false (Crane,

---

[7] Cognitive integration in the visual system is related to the matching of the novel object representations with the stored object representations in visual memory. This process is fundamental for object recognition. Further details on visual cognitive integration can be found in chapter one and chapter three of this work.

1992a). Illusions are a common example of visual misperception (Treisman and Schmitd, 1982; Robertson 2003). For example, 'illusory conjunction' occurs when the visual system erroneously conjoins features, resulting in a wrong representation of the object properties in a scene. I have shown that the structure behind veridical and illusory perception (at least in the case of illusory conjunction) is a systematic and compositional structure of constituents.

Thus, vision and thought are both representational systems. Representational systems, *qua* representational, describe the way the world is, namely, they are *world-directed* or *intentional*. A representation is intentional, if it is related to an object or property in the world. Whether thought is intentional and how to explain its intentionality is a matter of debate (Churchland, 1979; Churchland, P.S., 1986; Dennett, 1987; Fodor, 1987), and so it is the intentionality of the sensory systems (Akins, 1996). By stipulating that thought and vision are intentional, I want briefly to consider whether the intentionality of visual perception is like the intentionality of thought.

The answer is no: The intentionality of vision differs from the intentionality of thought (Clark, 2000; Lievers, 2005). Thought and perception have distinct ways to represent the world. This distinction has been described at length in this work, and it can be so summarized: Thought requires mental representations with conceptual content; instead vision requires processes on non-conceptual mental representations. A subject's belief that there is a red apple involves the subject to be in a computational/functional relation with a mental representation that expresses the object of the belief, namely, that there is a red apple. In order to be able to be in that state, one has to represent the apple *as* the apple. Representing something *as* involves the possession of the corresponding concepts: One can believe that there is a red apple only if one represents the apple and red as falling under the concepts APPLE and RED. On the opposite, the *aboutness* of the visual system involves a relation among visual representations and object properties in the world. This relation does not result in the possession of the concept for the represented properties but in their non-conceptual representation. Notice that the sensory representation of the world is often related to our ability to describe, judge, and have knowledge of things in the world. Thus, the informational exchange between the visual and conceptual systems has to support a way to transform non-conceptual representations into conceptual one.

Does differences in intentionality require a difference in structure? Probably yes, since the conceptual and visual systems seem to combine constituents according to different rules. The former has a language-like structure, while the latter combine constituents according to their spatial relations. This combinatorial difference might explain the difference in content between the representations in higher-cognitive systems and the ones in perceptual systems. Nevertheless, I would like to stress once more that from the fact that these systems have different structures, it does not follows that one of these system has a non-systematic and non-compositional structure. Specifically, I argue that vision has the same systematic and compositional properties that conceptual systems seems to have.

5.5 Conclusions

I argued that the visual representations involved in binding processes have a compositional structure of constituents. The explanation of how the content of visual representations composes relies on the argument for the systematicity of binding processes: Structurally related visual object representations share the same constituents that contribute with the same content to the content of the whole.

The importance of this approach is to render explicit that mental representations compose independently of their content (i.e., independently of their conceptual content). It turned out that the principle of (syntactic) compositionality of non-conceptual mental representations differs from previous accounts of the compositionality of mental representations, such as Fodor's account, because it does not require any constraint on theories of content possession. Because of this, the principle of syntactic compositionality is not threatened by the risk to be a vacuous theory, as a deflationary account of compositionality is.

A possible problem for my approach might arise from the fact that compositionality is seen as a semantic requirement. Thus, one might argue that there is no compositionality of non-conceptual representations. As described above, one cannot apply the classical definition of compositionality to visual processes, exactly because of their non-conceptual nature. But note that, the interesting part of this work is to show that the content of non-conceptual representations compose in a way that satisfy at least the requirement of syntactic compositionality. It is interesting to analyze how from this 'primitive' form of composition, more complex compositions (i.e., compositions of conceptual representations) derive. This analysis involves the study of how sensory systems (non-conceptual systems) interact with conceptual systems. One of the results of such an interaction is the transformation of non-conceptual representations into conceptual ones. How this transformation is achieved is an open question that deserves further studies on both the theoretical and empirical sides.

6
The Structure of Vision

As argued in previous chapters, vision as a parallel-distributed and hierarchical system combines primitive representations, so that structurally related object representations involve the same constituents (systematicity), and the content of those representations depends on the content of their primitive constituents (syntactic compositionality). The analysis of the structure of vision contrasts with already mentioned views in philosophy, according to which systematicity (and the related compositionality) is a lawful relation between certain abilities within the conceptual realm (Evans, 1982; McLaughlin, 2009). For example, the justification of the Generality Constraint is motivated by the fact that in order to entertain structurally related thoughts is necessary to possess the relevant concepts. As a consequence, visual representations, qua non-conceptual representations, lack a systematic and compositional structure of constituents (Clark, 2004b).

I argued instead for a systematic lawful relation between non-conceptual representations occurring during visual binding operations. In order to consider whether visual object representations have a systematic and compositional structure, I investigated whether phenomenal related visual scenes share the same constituents at the level of brain processes. In fact, it is not sufficient to state that a subject phenomenally perceives structurally related visual scenes: Similarities at the phenomenal level have to be accompanied by similarities at the level of the underlying representational processes. This requirement is necessary to characterize whether a system has a combinatorial structure of constituents that satisfies both compositionality and systematicity.

In this chapter, I would like to propose a further implication of characterizing vision as a system with a systematic structure of constituents. Given the similarities between the structure of thought and the structure of vision, what is the relation between those structures? Does the structure of thought mirror the structure of vision?

6.1 The Information-Link Between Demonstratives and Vision

Thought and visual perception are tightly related: Perception often provides information that is the ground for perceptual thoughts, such as, for example, perceptual demonstratives. Perceptual demonstratives, like the thoughts 'This is an apple', 'That is a tree', and so on, identify and refer to objects due to the information provided by sensory systems: Because of seeing and touching, for example, an apple, one can demonstratively indentify the object that is seeing and touching *as an apple*. The information-link between sensory information and thought is necessary to sustain demonstrative identification (Strawson, 1963).

Nevertheless, Evans (1982, ch. 6) argues that those information-links are not sufficient to sustain demonstrative identification, though they are necessary. This is because of the requirements a thought has to meet in order to satisfy the Generality Constraint. For the Generality Constraint, the identification of an object is related with the systematic ability to produce an indefinite number of thoughts about that specific object. If demonstrative thoughts only relied on the ongoing information presented by the senses, then a subject could entertain only those thoughts about the perceived objects. Instead, Evans noticed that humans are able to entertain an indefinite variety of thoughts once they possess the appropriate concepts. Concepts possession explains why human thoughts are essentially structured. In fact, Evans' justification of the Generality Constraint – or the claim that thoughts are structured – presupposes a fundamental level of conceptual abilities, more primitive than perceptual-based concepts that are necessary to identify the perceived objects. Thus, non-conceptual sensory information mainly plays a role in the causal explanation of how we are able to discriminate an object, belonging to a particular natural kind, of which we already possess a conception. Therefore, even if Evans' work was fundamental in the development of theories about non-conceptual content, in his work he supported a sort of conceptual realism (Lievers, 2005).

Both the claim that non-conceptual content is not sufficient for perceptual experience, and the appeal to a fundamental level of thought to justify the claim that thoughts are structured can be questioned.

An early critic of the conceptual content of visual experience seems to be implicitly contained in Jackson's description of the phenomenal sense of the word 'looks' (Jackson, 1977). The phenomenal use of 'looks' (i.e., 'It looks F to me') does not seem to involve concept possession for a subject to perceive the object of her perception. In this sense, the content of visual experience might be thought as being non-conceptual. In recent years, the argument of the conceptual nature of conscious visual experience has been challenged on the basis of different arguments supporting the non-conceptual content of visual experience.

- Structural differences (Heck, 2007): Vision and thought have distinct structures of constituents. Differences in the way the constituents are combined result in having different contents.
- Fineness of grain (Tye, 2006): The content of visual experience is too detailed to be fully captured by a description of what is visually represented
- Belief-independency (Jackson, 1977; Crane, 1992a): The content of visual experience is sometimes resistant to our beliefs, such as during perceptual illusions.
- Autonomy thesis (Bermúdez, 1994; Peacocke, 2002): There is no need to have a rich conceptual apparatus in order to have visual experience of the world.

The argument relies on the fact that human infants and animals have visual experience while lacking the conceptual apparatus of human adults.

The author mentioned above support the view that non-conceptual information is the content of sensory experience. This content is necessary and sufficient to identify objects in the world; hence, there is no need to postulate further conceptual abilities to sustain our experience of the world. The claim of the necessity of a fundamental level of thought to justify the structure of thought has thus been criticized. Authors like, for example, Campbell (2002) and Lievers (2005) argue that Evans' justification of the claim that thoughts are structured (i.e., the Generality Constraint) within the conceptual realm is too demanding. It does not seem necessary to posit a conceptual level that is more fundamental than the level of perceptual demonstratives that directly refer to objects in the world. Rather, thoughts about objects have to be considered the most basic kind of thoughts we posses. In this context, knowledge of the referent of a demonstrative does not depend on a subject's conceptual abilities but on the direct link between the perceived object and the demonstrative. Thus, reference to an object is not only caused by sensory information but also grounded on it.

This claim is supported by a casual account of knowledge of reference (Pyly-shyn, 2007; Raftopoulos and Muller, 2006). According to it, the relation between perception and objects in the world should be sought at the level of the direct causal relation between perception and the world. This means that there is so no intermediate conceptual level that determines the content of perceptual demonstratives. Hence, reference to objects emerges in conceptually unmediated ways from our viewing a scene. Causal theories of reference postulate, similar to Evans, that a selective mechanism is fundamental to determine knowledge of reference:

> Given that the existence of an information-link between subject and object is not by itself sufficient for identification, what makes it possible to have, in the standard case of demonstrative identification, a mode of identification that is free of the conceptual element we have been considering? The answer is that in the standard cases, not only is there an information-link, but also the subject can, upon the basis of that link, *locate the object in space*. (Evans, 1982, p. 150; *italics GE*).

The ability to locate an object in space is often coupled with an attentional mechanism. Theories of reference based on causal accounts focus on both object-based (Matthen, 2006; Pylyshyn, 2007) and space-based attention (Campbell, 2006a), reflecting researches at the heart of the Multiple-Object Tracking paradigm and Feature Integration Theory. I already considered the relation between visual binding operation and reference in chapter four. There, I argued that, independently of which kind of attention is postulated, attention seems to be a necessary mechanism to secure identity. For example, Clark (2004a) describes visual feature binding as a form of proto-reference, similar to Strawson's 'feature placing language' (Strawson, 1954, 1963, 1974), in which the terms referred by a demonstrative are predicates of a specific location, such as for example, 'Here it is vertical and red'. However, in Clark's account visual reference is dependent on sortal classification; that is to say, dependent on conceptual abilities (Campbell, 2006b).

Within the frame of object-based attention and consistent with a causal approach to reference, Pylyshyn (2007) recognizes the unifying role of attention, without invoking conceptual abilities. He suggests that the link between binding processes and demonstrative thoughts depends on the existence of an indexing mechanism (FINST) that tracks objects over time. This indexing mechanism occurs at early stages of the visual processing that are prior to conceptual experience, and is probably controlled by attention. The role of attention is to select an individual, discriminate the features belonging to it, and then binding those features to create a coherent representation of the attended object. The information retained during the indexing process is probably the kind of information that is at the basis of demonstrative thoughts. Actually, Pylyshyn considers the indexing mechanism to work as a demonstrative: Once we focus upon an object, and internal mental representation is formed, whose content is causally related to the object and its features. The selected visual information is relevant to determine the object of reference, when asked what we are attending to. If this is the case, then, at the sensory level, there is no need to possess concepts to identify the reference of a term in a demonstrative. Hence, indexing is a primitive and non-conceptual type of reference, or, proto-reference: The visual system does not represent a scene containing three apples *as containing three apples*, instead it only represents what and where is in a scene. Yet, since this primitive binding process is necessary for the later conceptual identification of objects, it can be considered as partly responsible for object identification.

If one supports the idea that cognition is inherently perceptual (Prinz, 2002), then the contribution of sensory experience plays a fundamental role in the determination of the conceptual realm. Barsalou (1999) claims that perception and cognition share systems and processes, such that similar properties arise. He particularly mentions that perceptual representations selected via an attentional mechanism stand for referents in the world, and enter into symbol recombination at the conceptual level. I have argued that the properties that underlie symbol manipulation within higher cognition are similar to the ones underlying the combination that leads to perceptual representations. Given the direct link between perception and cognition, can we justify the claim that thoughts are structured without positing an intermediate level of more fundamental conceptual abilities?

6.2 Reference and Visual Binding

In Campbell (2004), the ability to locate and identify objects depends on two related processes: conscious attention, and the brain processes underlying object representation. The role of conscious attention is to define the targets of brain processing, so that when a subject is focusing on an object, a certain kind of information is selected. Particularly, in the case of demonstrative identification, only information relevant to identify the referred object is selected. Thus, for example, if one wants to pick up a specific apple, then the brain processes encoding information to complete that task will be at work. In these terms, conscious attention affects (enhances) the underlying neuronal processes, resulting in the representation of the object of the demonstrative. Thus, conscious experience of an object provides subjects with knowledge of the referent of the demonstrative by overtly focusing, and highlighting a determined object in experience. This is achieved only if conscious experience and the underlying neuronal processes are related:

> If the singling-out of an object at the level of conscious experience is to be capable of affecting which information is to be singled out for further processing, at the level of the visual system, then there must be a commensurability between the way in which objects are identified at the level of conscious experience and the way in which objects are identified at the level of the underlying information-processing. (Campbell, 2004, p. 270).

The commensurability between identification at the level of conscious and non-conscious processes is given by the fact that the same mechanism is required to integrate and pick up information both at the informational and conscious level. Attention allows at the level of conscious visual experience for highlighting an object at a specific location and singling it out from other objects. At the same time, the same mechanism allows, at the level of binding operations, the integration of different features that occur at the same location in order to build up an object representation. Campbell, thus, suggests that "the principle used in solving the Binding Problem may also be used, in reverse now, to recover the right information from the underlying individual processing streams (Campbell, 2004, p. 272)."

Demonstrative identification depends on the activation by conscious attention of brain routines (i. e., the processes involved in visual feature binding) that recover the information about the referred object: If one thinks 'That apple', then one consciously attends to that specific apple, and, by attending to it, information in the feature maps relevant to the representation APPLE is picked out. Therefore, "the principle used in solving the binding problem provides a characterization of the meaning of a demonstrative referring to the object (Campbell, 2004, p. 272)." According to this, the information-link between visual processes and conscious visual experience seems to be not only necessary but also sufficient to identify an object.

Demonstrative thoughts, through attention, have, thus, a direct information-link with early binding operations: Whenever a subject is able to identify an object, visual features that belong to that object are selected and bound. Let us consider, for example, two demonstrative thoughts such as 'This is a red-vertical line' and 'That is a green-horizontal line'. Those thoughts receive inputs from the visual system, which represents the scene with the two distinct lines by the activation of the corresponding feature maps. In order to properly combine visual primitive features, an attentional mechanism selects features at a specific location (in the case of visual binding across feature dimensions), and integrates them in a way that can be described as 'At loc_i is red and vertical', and 'At loc_j is green and horizontal'.

As described in chapter four, we know that structurally related visual scenes share the same constituents, so that visual binding operations are systematic. This means that structurally related demonstrative thoughts depend on structurally related binding operations underling the representation of the object that is the referent of the demonstrative. If the information-link between sensory and demonstrative thought is necessary and sufficient to identify an object, then the structure of thought might directly mirror the systematic structure of visual object binding: We are able to identify the object in 'This is a red-vertical line' and 'That is a green-horizontal line', and to identify structurally related recombinations of those thoughts, because the identification of the terms in the demonstratives depends on the representation and integration of primitive features during binding processes. Thus, the claim that thought are structured might be justified by directly considering the structure of early sensory processing, thus, dissolving the further requirement of a fundamental level of thought. The same argument applies for the visual representation of extended objects (i. e., objects that occupy ample portions of the visual field), and for second-order binding (i. e., the representation of spatial relations between objects).

The case of second-order binding is particularly interesting in the context of demonstrative identification. I argued that the systematicity of second-order binding derives from the systematicity of visual feature binding (first-order binding), since the same mechanisms (i. e., attention and synchrony) that are involved in first-order binding are also involved in the representation of objects that are spatially related. However, I theorized that spatial relations between objects are implicitly represented by the visual system. That is to say, the visual system represents, for example, both an apple and a basket at their locations but might not explicitly represent, for example, the relation 'to the left of', in order to represent 'the apple is to the left of a basket'. I argued that information about spatial relations that is implicitly represented in vision is, instead, explicitly used by other systems, such as, for example, the motor system and higher-cognitive systems.

Now, I would like to propose a theoretical argument, according to which demonstrative thoughts, as visual second-order binding, do not explicitly represent spatial relations between the objects they identify. For example, to identify the object of the demonstrative 'That apple' in a scene that contains an apple to the left of a basket, we only need to identify where the apple is located, independently of its relative position to the basket. The relative position of the apple in respect of other objects becomes important (and, thus, explicitly represented) only when we describe a scene with multiple objects. If this is correct, then second-order binding provides a further argument for the necessity and sufficiency of visual information to secure object identification. In fact, demonstrative identification refers to an object mainly by selecting its location. I argued that information of where an object is located is probably represented in vision by exploiting the information about location as represented within feature maps and the saliency map. Information about an object location is, thus, coded within the visual system, and, through attention, exploited to identify an object while entertaining a demonstrative thought. Thus, information provided by the visual system is necessary and sufficient, in order to demonstratively identify an object.

To conclude: Given the relation between attention and reference, and since visual binding operations are systematic, one can argue that the systematicity of thought (at least, the systematicity of perceptual thought) mirrors the systematic structure of vision.

6.3 Conclusion

Thought and visual processes share structural properties, so that systematicity and compositionality are not only pervasive features of higher-level cognition but also features of sensory representational processes. This sentence can be interpreted in two ways: (i) According to a narrow interpretation, the visual representational system, as higher-cognitive systems, has a structure of constituents and the visual system is systematic and compositional; and (ii) according to a broad interpretation, systematicity and compositionality are pervasive features of all representational systems (i. e., all the sensory and higher-level cognitive systems) with a combinatorial structure.

My work does not provide an argument to sustain the broad interpretation. In fact, I did not consider whether sensory systems other than vision have a combinatorial structure of constituents. For this reason, even if the broad interpretation posits a valid inquiry about the possibility that systematicity and compositionality are pervasive features of combinatorial processes in different sensory modalities, this hypothesis needs further evidence to be tested.

Instead, I have extensively described the structure of vision, in a way that justifies the narrow interpretation. Specifically, in this chapter I focused on the relation between perceptual thought and vision, and posited the question of whether the systematic structure of constituents in thought depends on the influence of early sensory processes, by considering the role of attention in securing identity both in visual feature binding and in demonstrative identification. I do not have a conclusive argument on the relation of dependency of those structures; namely, it is still unclear whether it is the structure of thought that mirrors the structure of early visual processes or vice versa. For the moment, I can only argue for a broadening of the Generality Constraint, such that it describes a general property of the thought and visual systems, and not only a fundamental property of thought.

Conclusions

The visual system provides us with experience and knowledge of the external world. The ongoing flow of information that reaches the retina is filtered and combined so that we can identify the different objects in a visual scene. Evidence from vision science reports that the representation of a visual scene depends on parallel and structured processes, which involve the combination of primitive representations. The aim of this work was to investigate what are the properties underlying visual combinatorial processes in order to evaluate if vision is systematic and compositional. I, specifically, focused on the structure of visual binding operations by integrating philosophical insights into the properties of combinatorial and representational systems with psychophysical and neuroscientific studies of visual feature binding.

On the one hand, the philosophical literature on the structure of mental representations revolves around a specific topic: Combinatorial mental representations have a systematic and compositional structure of constituents. This particular structure is typical of symbolic and serial systems like the 'thought system' but is precluded to any non-conceptual and parallel-distributed system (as argued by Evans with the postulation of the Generality Constraint, and by Fodor's Language of Thought theory).

On the other hand, studies in vision science describe visual object representation as a structured process. Specifically, the solution of the binding problem in vision necessitates an active mechanism that integrates features according to the object they belong to. An attentional mechanism seems to be fundamental to actively bind visual features: According to Feature Integration Theory of attention (FIT), attention selects a specific object and integrates features that occur at the same location. I also proposed that the synchronous activity of neurons that represent features belonging to the same object (as described by the hypothesis of binding by synchrony) might correspond to the neuronal implementation of the attentional mechanism, instead of being a completely distinct binding mechanism. Evidence for an active binding mechanism allowed me to evaluate which structure is imposed on feature processing in order to represent an object. I suggested that the representation of feature locations within visual feature maps plays a fundamental role in explaining the systematicity of the binding process. Systematicity results from the fact that structurally related visual scenes involve the activation of the same features but at different locations. Features are, then, combined differently, according to the location where they occur. This combination gives rise to novel representations. I mainly considered the hypothesis of binding by attention but I extended my research on other binding mechanisms, as well. I could explain the systematicity of perceptual grouping and second-order binding (i.e., how spatial relations between objects in a visual scene are represented), by extending my analysis of the processes underlying visual feature binding (first-order binding).

Since systematicity often presupposes compositionality, I investigated whether the principle of semantic compositionality applies to visual processes. Because of the non-conceptual nature of visual representations, a deflationary account of compositionality – the principle of syntactic compositionality – is necessary to explain how the contents of visual representations compose.

Thus, vision and thoughts share similar structured properties, even if they combine constituents according to different rules. Since perceptual thoughts, and, specifically, visual demonstratives, are tightly linked to visual processes, I proposed that the Generality Constraint does not only describe a distinguished characteristic of thought; rather, it describes a general structure of cognitive processes.

To conclude, my work provides a strong argument for the visual system as being a systematic and compositional system with a causal structure of constituents. Since vision is a highly parallel and hierarchical system, I also provide a strong argument for the systematicity and compositionality of parallel-distributed models of early sensory processes.

References

Akins, K. (1996). Of Sensory Systems and the "Aboutness" of Mental States. *The Journal of Philosophy*, 93: 337–372.

Barlow, H.B. (1972). Single units and sensation: A neuron doctrine for perceptual psychology? *Perception*, 1: 371–394.

Barsalou, L.W. (1992). Frames, Concepts, and Conceptual Fields. In A. Lehrer and E. F. Kittay, (Eds.), *Frames, Fields, and Contrasts*, Hillsdale: Lawrence Erlbaum Associates, 21–74.

– (1999). Perceptual Symbol Systems. *Behavioral and Brain Sciences*, 22: 577–660.

Barsalou, L.W., Prinz J.J. (1997). Mundane creativity in perceptual symbol systems. In T.B. Ward, S.M. Smith, J. Vaid, (Eds.), *Creative thought: An investigation of conceptual structures and processes*, Washington, DC: American Psychological Association, 267–307.

Barsalou, L.W., Simmons W.K., Barbey A.K., Wilson C.D. (2003). Grounding conceptual knowledge in modality-specific systems. *Trends in Cognitive Sciences*, 7: 84–91.

Bermúdez, J.L. (1994). Peacocke's argument against the autonomy of nonconceptual representational content. *Mind and Language*, 9: 402–418.

– (1995). Nonconceptual Content: From Perceptual Experience to Subpersonal Computational States. *Mind and Language*, 10: 333–369.

Biederman, I. (1987). Recognition-by-components: A theory of human image interpretation. *Psychological Review*, 94: 115–148.

Bienenstock E., Geman S. (1995). Compositionality in Neural Systems. In M. Arbib, (Ed.), *The Handbook of Brain Theory and Neural Networks*, Cambridge (MA): MIT Press, 223–226.

Blaser, E., Papathomas, T., Vidnyanszky, Z. (2005). Binding of motion and colour is early and automatic. *European Journal of Neuroscience*, 21: 2040–2044.

Blaser, E., Pylyshyn Z.P., Holcombe, A.O. (2000). Tracking an object through feature-space. *Nature*, 408: 196–199.

Campbell, J. (2002) *Reference and Consciousness*. Oxford University Press.

– (2004). Reference as Attention. *Philosophical Studies*, 120: 265–276.

– (2006a). Does visual attention depends on sortal classification? Reply to Clark. *Philosophical Studies*, 127: 221–237.

– (2006b). What is the role of location in the sense of a visual demonstrative? Reply to Matthen. *Philosophical Studies*, 127: 239–254.

Chisholm, M. (1957). *Perceiving: A Philosophical Study*. Ithaca (NY): Cornell University Press.

Chomsky, N. (1965). *Aspects of the Theory of Syntax*. Cambridge (MA): MIT Press.

Churchland, P. (1979). *Scientific Realism and the Plasticity of Mind*. Cambridge: Cambridge University Press.

Churchland, P.S. (1986). *Neurophilosophy: Toward a Unified Science of the Mind-Brain*. Cambridge (MA): MIT Press.

Clark, Andy (1991). Systematicity, structured representations and cognitive architecture: A reply to Fodor and Pylyshyn. In T. Horgan, J. Tienson, (Eds.), *Connectionism and the Philosophy of Mind*, Dordrecht: Kluwer Academy Publishers, 198–218.

- (1993). *Associative Engines*. Cambridge (MA): MIT Press.

Clark, Austen (1993). *Sensory Qualities*. Oxford University Press.

- (2000). *A theory of sentience*. Oxford: Oxford University Press.

- (2001). Some logical features of feature integration. In W. Backhaus, (Ed.), *Neuronal Coding of Perceptual Systems*, New Jersey: World Scientific, 3–20.

- (2004a). Feature-placing and proto-objects. *Philosophical Psychology*, 17: 443–469.

- (2004b). Sensing, objects, and awareness: reply to commentators. *Philosophical Psychology*, 17: 553–579.

Crane, T. (1988). The waterfall illusion. *Analysis*, 48: 142–147.

- (1992a). The nonconceptual content of experience. In T. Crane (Ed.), *The Contents of Experience: Essays on perception*. Cambridge: Cambridge University Press.

- (1992b). *The Contents of Experience: Essays on perception*. Cambridge: Cambridge University Press.

Cohen, J. (2004a). Objects, Places, and Perception, *Philosophical Psychology*, 17: 471–495.

- (2004b). Information and Content. In L. Floridi, (Ed.), *Blackwell Guide to the Philosophy of Information and Computing*, New York: Blackwell, 215–227.

Condillac, Étienne Bonnot de (1980). *La Logique/Logic*. W.R. Albury, (Ed. and Trans.), New York: Abaris.

Crick, F., Koch, C. (1990). Towards a neurobiological theory of consciousness. *Seminars in The Neurosciences*, 2: 273–304.

- (1995). Are we aware of neural activity in primary visual cortex? *Nature*, 375: 121–123.

Dennett, D.C. (1987). *The Intentional Stance*. Cambridge (MA): MIT Press.

Drestke, F.I. (1981). *Knowledge and the Flow of Information*. Cambridge (MA): MIT Press.

- (1988). *Explaining behavior: Reasons in a World of Causes*. Cambridge (MA): MIT Press.

- (1995). *Naturalizing the Mind*. Cambridge (MA): MIT Press.

Dummett, M. (1981). *The interpretation of Frege's philosophy*. London: Duckworth.

Edelman, S. (1997). Computational theories of object recognition. *Trends in Cognitive Sciences*, 1: 296–304.

- (2002). Constraints on the nature of the neural representation of the visual world. *Trends in Cognitive Sciences*, 6: 125–131.

Edelman, S., Intrator, I. (2003). Toward structural systematicity in distributed, statically bound visual representations. *Cognitive Science*, 27: 73–109.

Engel, A.K., Kreiter, A.K., König, P., Singer, W. (1991). Synchronization of oscillatory neuronal responses between striate and extrastriate visual cortical areas of the cat. *PNAS*, 88: 6048–6052.

Engel, A.K., Singer, W. (2001). Temporal binding and the neural correlates of sensory awareness. *Trends in Cognitive Sciences*, 5:16–25.

Evans, G. (1982). *The Varieties of Reference*. New York: Oxford University Press.

Felleman, D.J., Van Essen, D.C. (1991). Distributed Hierarchical Processing in the Primate Cerebral Cortex. *Cerebral Cortex*, 1: 1–47.

Fodor, J.A. (1975). *The Language of Thought*. New York: Crowell.

- (1987). *Psychosemantics: The Problem of Meaning in the Philosophy of Mind*. Cambridge (MA): MIT Press.
- (1990). *A Theory of Content and Other Essays*. Cambridge (MA): MIT Press.
- (1996). Connectionism and the problem of systematicity (continued): Why Smolensky's solution still doesn't work. *Cognition*, 62: 109–119.
- (1998a). *Concepts: Where Cognitive Science Went Wrong*. Oxford: Clarendon Press.
- (1998b). *In Critical Condition: Polemical Essays on Cognitive Science and the Philosophy of Mind*. Cambridge (MA): MIT Press.
- (2001). Language, Thought and Compositionality. *Mind and Language*, 16: 1–15.
- (2007). The Revenge of the Given. In B.P. McLaughlin, J. Cohen, (Eds.), *Contemporary Debates in Philosophy of Mind*, Blackwell Publishing, 105–116.

Fodor, J.A., Lepore, E. (2001) Why Compositionality Won't Go Away: Reflections on Horwich's 'Deflationary' Theory. *Ratio*, 14: 350–368.

Fodor, J.A., McLaughlin, B.P. (1990). Connectionism and the Problem of Systematicity: Why Smolensky's Solution doesn't Work. *Cognition*, 35: 183–204.

Fodor, J.A., Pylyshyn, Z.W. (1988). Connectionism and cognitive architecture: A critical analysis. *Cognition*, 28: 3–71.

Frank, S. L., Haselager, W.F.G., van Rooij I. (2009). Connectionist semantic systematicity. *Cognition*, *110*, 358–379.

Frege, G. (1879/1967). *Begriffsschrift, eine der arithmetischen nachgebildete Formelsprache des reinen Denkens*. Halle a. S.: Louis Nebert. S. Bauer-Mengelberg, (Trans.), *Concept Script, a formal language of pure thought modelled upon that of arithmetic*. In J. vanHeijenoort, (Ed.), *From Frege to Gödel: A Source Book in Mathematical Logic, 1879–1931*, Cambridge, MA: Harvard University Press, 1–82.

- (1892/1952). Über Sinn und Bedeutung. *Zeitschrift für Philosophie und philosophische Kritik*, 100: 25–50. Translated as On sense and reference, in P. Geach, M. Black, (Eds.), *Translations from the Philosophical Writings of Gottlob Frege*. Oxford: Blackwell, 56–78.
- (1914). Logic in mathematics. P. Long, R.White (Trans.), in Hermes et al., (Eds.), *Gottlob Frege: Posthumous Writings*, Chicago: University of Chicago Press, 203–252.
- (1918/1967). Der Gedanke. Eine Logische Untersuchung. In *Beiträge zur Philosophie des deutschen Idealismus* I. Translated as Thoughts: A Logical Enquiry, in P. Strawson, (Ed.), *Philosophical Logic*, London: Oxford University Press, 17–38.

Friedman-Hill, S.R., Robertson, L.C., Treisman, A. (1995). Parietal contributions to visual feature binding: evidence from a patient with bilateral lesions. *Science*, 269: 853–855.

Fries, P., Reynolds, J.H., Rorie, A.E., Desimone, R. (2001) Modulation of oscillatory activity by selective visual attention. *Science*, 291: 1560–1563.

Gendler, T.S., Hawthorne, J. (2006). *Perceptual Experience*. Oxford University Press.

Gilbert, C.D., Sigman, M. (2007). Brain states: Top-down influences in sensory processing. *Neuron*, *54:* 677–696.

Gottlieb, G. (2007). From thought to action: The parietal cortex as a bridge between perception, action, and cognition. *Neuron*, *53*, 9–16.

Gray, C.M. (1999). The Temporal Correlation Hypothesis of Visual Feature Integration: Still Alive and Well. *Neuron*, 24: 31–47.

Gray, C.M., Engel, A.K., König P., Singer W. (1989). Oscillatory responses in cat visual cortex exhibit inter-columnar synchronization which reflects global stimulus properties. *Nature*, 338: 334–337.

Gray, C.M., Singer, W. (1989). Stimulus-specific neuronal oscillations in orientation columns of cat visual cortex. *PNAS*, 86: 1698–1702.

Grill-Spector, K., Malach, R. (2004). The human visual cortex. *Annual Review Neuroscience*, 27: 649–677.

Hardcastle, V.G. (1994). Psychology's Binding Problem and Possible Neurobiological Solutions. *Journal of Consciousness Studies*, 1: 66–90.

Hayworth, K., Lescroart, M., Biederman, I. (2008). Explicit relation coding in the Lateral Occipital Complex. *Journal of Vision*, 8 (6), 35, from http://journalofvision.org/8/6/35/.

Hebb, D.O. (1949). *The organization of behavior: A neuropsychological theory*. Wiley.

Heck, R.G. (2000). Nonconceptual content and the "space of reasons". *Philosophical Review* 109: 483–523.

– (2007). Are There Different Kinds of Content? In B.P. McLaughlin, J. Cohen, (Eds.), *Contemporary Debates in Philosophy of Mind*, Blackwell Publishing, 117–138.

Hinton, G.E., McClelland, J.L., Rummelhart, D.E. (1986). Distributed representations. In D.E. Rummelhart, J.L. McClelland, and the PDP Research Group (Eds.), *Parallel Distributed Processing, Vol. 1,* Cambridge (MA): MIT Press, 77–109.

Horwich, P. (1997). The Composition of Meanings. *Philosophical Review*, 106: 503–532.

– (1998). *Meaning*. Oxford: Clarendon Press.

– (2001). Deflating Compositionality. *Ratio*, 14: 369–385.

– (2005). *Reflections on Meaning*. New York: Oxford University Press.

Hubel, D.H., Wiesel, T.N. (1968). Receptive fields and functional architecture of monkey striate cortex. *Journal of Physiology*, 195: 215–243.

Hummel, J.E. (2000). Where view-based theories break down: The role of structure in shape perception and object recognition. In E. Dietrich, A. Markman (Eds.), *Cognitive dynamics: Conceptual change in humans and machines* (pp. 157–185). Mahwah, NJ: Erlbaum.

– (2001). Complementary solutions to the binding problem in vision: Implications for shape perception and object recognition. *Visual Cognition*, 8: 489–517.

Hummel, J.E., Biederman, I. (1992). Dynamic binding in a neural network for shape recognition. *Psychological Review*, 99: 480–517.

Humphreys, G.W., Riddoch, M.J. (2006). Features, objects, action: The cognitive neuropsychology of visual object processing, 1984–2004. *Cognitive Neuropsychology*, 23: 156–183.

Itti, L., Koch, C. (2001). Computational modelling of visual attention. *Nature Reviews Neuroscience*, 2: 194–203.

Jackendoff, R. (2002). *Foundations of Language. Brain, Meaning, Grammar, Evolution*. Oxford University Press.

Jackson, F. (1977). *Perception: A Representative Theory*. Cambridge: Cambridge University Press.

James, W. (1890/1981). *The Principles of Psychology*. Cambridge: Harvard University Press.

Janssen, T.M.V. (1997). Compositionality. In T. van Benthem, A. ter Meulen, (Eds.), *Handbook of Logic and Language*, Amsterdam: Elsevier, and Cambridge (MA): MIT Press, 417–473.

Julesz, B. (1981). Textons, the elements of texture perception, and their interactions. *Nature*, 290: 91–97.

Kanizsa, G. (1979). *Organization in Vision: Essays on Gestalt Perception*. New York: Praeger Publishers.

Kant, I. (1787/1929). *Critique of Pure Reason*. N. Kemp Smith (Trans.), London: Macmillan.

Kastner, S., McMains, S.A. (2007). Out of the spotlight: face to face with attention. *Nature Neuroscience*, 10: 1344–1345.

Kazmi, A., Pelletier, F.J. (1998). Is compositionality vacuous? *Linguistics and Philosophy*, 21: 11–33.

Kelly, S.D. (2001). Demonstrative Concepts and Experience. *The Philosophical Review*, 110: 397–420.

Kitcher, P. (1990). *Kant's Transcendental Psychology*. New York: Oxford University Press.

Kitcher, P., Varzi, A. (2000). Some Pictures are Worth $2^\aleph{}_0$ Sentences. *Philosophy*, 75: 377–381.

Koch, C., Ullman, S. (1985). Shifts in selective visual attention: towards the underlying neural circuitry. *Human Neurobiology*, 4: 219–227.

Koffka, K. (1935). *Principles of Gestalt psychology*. New York: Harcourt, Brace & World.

Kosslyn, S.M. (1994). *Image and brain: The resolution of the imagery debate*. Cambridge (MA): MIT Press.

Kosslyn, S.M., Thompson W.L., Ganis, G. (2006). *The Case for Mental Imagery*. Oxford University Press.

Lamme, V.A.F., Spekreijse, H (1998). Neuronal synchrony does not represent texture segregation. *Nature,* 396: 362–366.

Lievers, M. (2005). The Structure of Thoughts. In M. Werning, E. Machery, G. Schurz, (Eds.), *The Compositionality of Meaning and Content. Volume 1: Foundational Issues*, Ontos Verlag, 169–188.

Locke, J. (1690/1975). *An Essay Concerning Human Understanding*. P.H. Nidditch (Ed.), Oxford: Clarendon Press.

Loewer, B., Rey, G. (1991), *Meaning in Mind: Fodor and his Critics*. Oxford: Blackwell.

Luck, S.J., Vogel, E.V. (1997). The capacity of visual working memory for features and conjunctions. *Nature*, 390: 279–281.

Machery, E., Werning, M., Schurz, G. (2005). *The Compositionality of Meaning and Content. Volume II: Applications to Linguistics, Psychology, and Neuroscience*, Ontos Verlag.

Marr, D. (1982). *Vision*. San Francisco: W.H. Freeman.

Marr, D., Nishihara, H.K. (1978). Representation and Recognition of Spatial Organization of Three-Dimensional Shapes. *Proceedings of the Royal Society of London B*, 200: 269–294.

Matthen, M. (2004). Features, places, and things: reflections on Austen Clark's theory of sentience. *Philosophical Psychology*, 17: 497–518.

– (2006). On visual experience of objects. *Philosophical Studies*, 127:195–220.

Matthews, R.J. (1997). Can Connectionists Explain Systematicity? *Mind and Language*, 12: 154–177.

McDowell, J. (1994). *Mind and World*. Cambridge (MA): Cambridge University Press.
- (1998a). Précis of Mind and World. *Philosophy and Phenomenological Research*, 58: 365–368.
- (1998b). Reply to Commentators. *Philosophy and Phenomenological Research*, 58: 403–431.
McLaughlin, B.P. (1993a). The Connectionism/Classicism Battle to Win Souls. *Philosophical Studies*, 71: 163–190.
- (1993b). Systematicity, Conceptual Truth, and Evolution. In C. Hookway, D. Peterson, (Eds.), *Philosophy and Cognitive Science*. Royal Institute of Philosophy, Supplement No. 34, 217–234.
- (2009). Systematicity Redux. *Synthese*, 170: 251–274.
McLaughlin, B.P., Cohen J. (2007). *Contemporary Debates in Philosophy of Mind*. Blackwell Publishing.
Millikan, R.G. (1984). *Language, Thought, and Other Biological Categories: New Foundations for Realism*. Cambridge (MA): MIT Press.
- (1986). Thought without laws: Cognitive science with content. *The Philosophical Review*, 95: 47–80.
- (1989). Biosemantics. *The Journal of Philosophy*, 86: 281–297.
Moran, J., Desimone, R. (1985). Selective attention gates visual processing in the extrastriate cortex. *Science*, 229: 782–784.
Odifreddi, P.G. (1999). *Classical Recursion Theory. Volume II*. North Holland.
Palanca, B.J.A., DeAngelis G.C. (2005). Does Neuronal Synchrony Underlie Visual Feature Grouping? *Neuron*, 46: 333–346.
Palmer, S.E. (1977). Hierarchical structure in perceptual representation. *Cognitive Psychology*, 9: 441–474.
Palmeri, T.J., Gauthier, I. (2004). Visual Object Understanding. *Nature Reviews Neuroscience*, 5: 291–304.
Peregrin, J. (2005). Is compositionality an Empirical Matter? In M. Werning, E. Machery, G. Schurz, (Eds.), *The Compositionality of Meaning and Content. Volume 1: Foundational Issues*, Ontos Verlag, 231–246.
Peacocke, C. (1986). Analogue Content. *Proceedings of the Aristotelian Society*, Supplementary Volume 60: 1–17.
- (1992a). *A Study of Concepts*. Cambridge, MA: MIT Press.
- (1992b). Scenarios, concepts and perception. In T. Crane, (Ed.), *The Contents of Experience: Essays on perception*. Cambridge: Cambridge University Press, 105–135.
- (1994). Nonconceptual content: kinds, rationale, relations. *Mind and Language*, 9: 419–429.
- (1998). Nonconceptual Content Defended. *Philosophy and Phenomenological Research*, 58: 381–88.
- (2001). Does Perception have a Nonconceptual Content? *The Journal of Philosophy*, 98: 239–64.
- (2002). Postscript to Peacocke 1994. In Y. Gunther, (Ed.), *Essays on nonconceptual content*, Cambridge (MA): MIT Press.
Pelletier, F.J. (1994). The Principle of Semantic Compositionality. *Topoi*, 13: 11–24.

– (2001). Did Frege Believe Frege's Principle? *Journal of Logic, Language, and Information*, 10: 87–114.

Pitcher, G. (1971). *A Theory of Perception*. New Jersey: Princeton University Press.

Prinz, J.J. (2002). *Furnishing the Mind: Concepts and Their Perceptual Basis*. Cambridge (MA): MIT Press.

Pylyshyn, Z.W. (1989). The role of location indexes in spatial perception: A sketch of FINST spatial-index model. *Cognition*, 32: 65–97.

– (2001). Visual indexes, preconceptual objects, and situated vision. *Cognition*, 80: 127–158.

– (2007). *Things and Places: How the Mind Connects with the World*. Cambridge (MA): MIT Press.

Pylyshyn, Z.W., Eagleson, R.A. (1994). Developing a network model of multiple visual indexing. *Investigative Ophthalmology and Visual Science*, 35: 2007–2007 (Abstract).

Pylyshyn, Z.W., Storm, R.W. (1988). Tracking multiple independent targets: evidence for a parallel tracking mechanism. *Spatial Vision*, 3: 1–19.

Qiu, F.T., Sugihara, T., von der Heydt, R. (2007). Figure-ground mechanisms provide structure for selective attention. *Nature Neuroscience*, 10: 1492–1499.

Raftopoulos, A., Muller, V. (2006). Nonconceptual Demonstrative Reference. *Philosophy and Phenomenological Research*, 2: 251–285.

Rao, S.C., Rainer, G., Miller E.K. (1997). Integration of What and Where in the Primate Prefrontal Cortex. *Science*, 276: 821–824.

Reynolds, J.H., Desimone, R. (1999) The role of neural mechanisms of attention in solving the binding problem. *Neuron*, 24: 19–29.

Riesenhuber, M., Poggio, T. (1999). Hierarchical models of object recognition in cortex. *Nature Neuroscience*, 2: 1019–1025.

Robertson, L.C. (2003). Binding, Spatial Attention and Perceptual Awareness. *Nature Reviews Neuroscience*, 4: 93–102.

Robinson, D.L., Petersen, S.E. (1992). The pulvinar and visual salience. *Trends in Neurosciences, 15*, 127–132.

Roskies, A.L. (1999). The Binding Problem. *Neuron*, 24: 7–11.

Salinas, E., Sejnowski, T.J. (2001). Correlated neuronal activity and the flow of neural information. *Nature Reviews Neuroscience, 2*: 539–550.

Schiffer, S. (1981). Truth and the Theory of Content. In H. Parret, J. Bouveresse, (Eds.), *Meaning and Understanding*, Berlin: de Gruyter.

– (1991). Does mentalese have a compositional semantics? In B. Loewer, G. Rey, (Eds.), *Meaning in Mind: Fodor and His Critics*, Oxford: Blackwell.

Scholl, B.J. (2009) What have we learned about attention from multiple object tracking (and vice versa)? In D. Dedrick L. Trick (Eds.), *Computation, cognition, and Pylyshyn* (pp. 49–78). Cambridge, MA: MIT Press.

Shadlen, M.N., Movshon, J.A. (1999). Synchrony unbound: a critical evaluation of the temporal binding hypothesis. *Neuron*, 24: 67–77.

Siegel, M., Donner, T.H., Oostenveld, R., Fries, P., Engel, A.K. (2008). Neuronal synchronization along the dorsal visual pathway reflects the focus of spatial attention. *Neuron, 60*, 709–719.

Singer, W. (1999). Neuronal synchrony: a versatile code for the definition of relations? *Neuron*, 24: 49–65.

Singer W., Gray, C.M. (1995). Visual feature integration and the temporal correlation hypothesis. *Annual Review Neuroscience*, 18: 555–586.

Smolensky, P. (1988). On the Proper Treatment of Connectionism. *Behavioral and Brain Sciences*, 11: 1–74.

–   (1990). Tensor Product, Variable Binding, and the Representation of Symbolic Structures in Connectionist Systems. *Artificial Intelligence*, 46: 159–216.

–   (1991). Connectionism, constituency, and the language of thought. In B. Loewer, G. Rey, (Eds.), *Meaning in Mind: Fodor and his Critics*. Oxford: Blackwell, 201–227.

Strawson, P.F. (1954). Particular and general. *Proceedings of the Aristotelian Society*, 54: 233–260.

–   (1963). *Individuals*. New York: Anchor Books.

–   (1974). *Subject and predicate in logic and grammar*. London: Methuen & Co. Lt

Szabó, Z.G. (2000). Compositionality as Supervenience. *Linguistics and Philosophy*, 23: 475–505.

Tarr, M.J., & Bülthoff, H.H. (1998). Image-based object recognition in man, monkey and machine. *Cognition*, 67, 1–20.

Thiele, A., Stoner, G. (2003). Neuronal synchrony does not correlate with motion coherence in cortical area MT. *Nature*, 421: 366–370.

Treisman, A.M. (1988). Features and objects: the fourteenth bartlett memorial lecture. *Quarterly Journal of Experimental Psychology*, 40 A: 201–237.

–   (1993). The perception of features and objects. In A. Baddeley, L. Weiskrantz, (Eds.), *Attention: Selection, Awareness, and Control*, Oxford: Clarendon Press, 1–36.

–   (1996). The binding problem. *Current Opinion Neurobiology*, 6: 171–178.

Treisman, A.M., Gelade, G. (1980). A feature–integration theory of attention. *Cognitive Psychology*, 12: 97–136.

Treisman, A.M., Schmidt, H. (1982). Illusory conjunctions in perception of objects. *Cognitive Psychology*, 14: 107–141.

Tye, M. (2000). *Consciousness, Color, and Content*. Cambridge (MA): MIT Press.

–   (2006). Nonconceptual Content, Richness, and Fineness of Grain. In T.S. Gendler and J. Hawthorne, (Eds.), *Perceptual Experience*, Oxford: Oxford University Press, 504–530.

Ungerleider, L. G., Mishkin, M. (1982). Two cortical visual systems. In D. J. Ingle, M. A. Goodale, R.J.W. Mansfield, (Eds.), *Analysis of visual behaviour*, Cambridge, MA: MIT Press, 549–585.

Von der Malsburg, C. (1981). The correlation theory of brain function. *Internal Report 81-2*, Max Planck Institute for Biophysical Chemistry, Göttingen, Germany.

–   (1987). Synaptic plasticity as basis of brain organization. In J.P. Changeux, M. Konishi, (Eds.), *The Neural and Molecular Bases of Learning*, New York: John Wiley and Sons, 411–432.

–   (1999). The What and Why of Binding: The Modeler's Perspective. *Neuron*, 24: 95–104.

Wandell, B.A., Brewer, A.A., Dougherty, R.F. (2005). Visual field map clusters in human cortex. *Philosophical Transactions of The Royal Society B*, 360: 693–707.

Wandell, B.A., Dumoulin, S.O., Brewer, A.A. (2007). Visual Field Maps in Human Cortex. *Neuron*, 56: 366–383.

Werning, M. (2003). Synchrony and composition: Toward a cognitive architecture between classicism and connectionism. In B. Löwe, W. Malzkorn, T. Raesch (Eds.), *Applications of mathematical logic in philosophy and linguistics* (pp. 261–278). Dordrecht: Kluwer.

– (2005). Neuronal Synchronization, Covariation, and Compositional Representation. In E. Machery, M. Werning, G. Schurz, (Eds.), *The Compositionality of Meaning and Content. Volume II: Applications to Linguistics, Psychology, and Neuroscience*, Ontos Verlag, 283–312.

Werning, M., Machery, E., Schurz, G. (2005). *The Compositionality of Meaning and Content. Volume 1: Foundational Issues*. Ontos Verlag.

Wertheimer, M. (1938). Gestalt theory. In W.D. Ellis (Ed. & Trans.), *A source book of Gestalt psychology* (pp. 1–11). London: Routledge & Kegan Paul.

Westerståhl, D. (1998). On mathematical proofs of the vacuity of compositionality. *Linguistics and Philosophy*, 21: 635–643.

Wolfe, J. (1994). Guided Search 2.0: A revised model of visual search. *Psychonomics Bulletin and Review*, 1: 202–238.

– (1998). Visual Search. In H.E. Pashler, (Ed.), *Attention*, London: Psychology Press, 13–73.

Wolfe, J.M., Bennett S.C. (1997). Preattentive object files: Shapeless bundles of basic features. *Vision Research, 37*, 25–43.

Wolfe, J., Cave, K.R. (1999). The Psychophysical Evidence for a Binding Problem in Human Vision. *Neuron*, 24: 11–17.

Wu, D., Kanai, R., Shimojo, S. (2004). Steady-state misbinding of colour and motion. *Nature*, 429: 262.

Zadrozny, W. (1994). From compositional to systematic semantics. *Linguistics and Philosophy*, 17: 329–342.

Zeki, S. (1978). Functional Specialization in the Visual Cortex of the Rhesus Monkey. *Nature*, 274: 423–428.

Index